Countdown to Crisis

2000

John G. Day 1997

OSCAR PUBLISHING
P.O. BOX 153
RAMSEY, NEW JERSEY 07446

THIS BOOK IS A WORK OF FICTION. NAMES, CHARACTERS, PLACES AND INCIDENTS ARE EITHER PRODUCTS OF THE AUTHOR'S IMAGINATION OR ARE USED FICTITIOUSLY. ANY RESEMBLANCE TO EVENTS OR LOCALES OR PERSONS LIVING OR DEAD IS ENTIRELY COINCIDENTAL.

COPYRIGHT © 1997 BY JOHN G. DAY

ALL RIGHTS RESERVED
INCLUDING THE RIGHT OF REPRODUCTION
IN WHOLE OR IN PART IN ANY FORM.

DESIGNED BY EDNA GREGORY
PRINTED IN THE United States of America

Library of Congress Catalog Card Number: 98-93949

CATALOGING IN PUBLICATION DATA

DAY, JOHN

COUNTDOWN TO CRISIS

ISBN: 1-893024-50-4

Printed in the USA by

MORRIS PUBLISHING

3212 East Highway 30 • Kearney, NE 68847 • 1-800-650-7888

To my wife Edna, son Jon and daughter Jill

With thanks for all their love and support.

Prologue

"Man, this reprogramming of the policy reimbursement system will never be done!" Bob Manners screamed to be heard over the jukebox's rendition of "Staying Alive," as he leaned against the bar and stared with unseeing eyes at the mirror facing him.

"It's going nowhere fast!" he continued and turned to look squarely at his friend and work colleague, Tony Willsen. Tony's concentration was centered on a small blonde woman who was trying to catch the elderly bartender's attention. Frustration contorted her face as the old man continually ignored her, preferring to serve the male customers first. Tony felt Bob's cold stare on the back of his neck as he raised a cold bottle of Budweiser, took a long drink, then smacked his lips.

"I'm listening!" he said emphatically and turned to face Bob who had an agitated look.

"You never heard a single thing!" Bob sneered, "You've only one thing on your mind!" he paused and glanced over at the blonde, raising his eyebrows. "How many times do you have to be refused?"

"No harm in trying!" Tony's shoulders sagged and his mouth hung open as he turned to concentrate on the blonde again.

She was about five foot six inches tall, with dyed stringy hair; pale complexion and a cute turned up nose. Her, short, red low cut dress, accentuated her large breasts. A slim waist, flat stomach and long legs, made shapely by thick dark nylons, gave her a provocative look, which promised much. Bob continued to shout above the music and general noise of the bar.

"This job's crazy, I don't know how you can stand it!" He looked around the dingy room; the darkened smoke filled atmosphere was depressing to anyone sober.

His gaze then drifted towards Tony again whose attention had remained fixed on the blonde as he watched her return to her girlfriend. She leant forward placing two full glasses of scotch down on the small table, sat down and crossed her legs. They both lifted their glasses and took a sip of their drinks, carefully scouring the room for potential company.

"The Office" was a popular old bar frequented by commuter's enroute to their suburban homes. It also doubled as a disco on Friday and Saturday nights and served half-priced drinks to unaccompanied women between 5.p.m and 8.p.m. This Friday night was not very busy and the jukebox substituted the absent DJ. Tony enjoyed the weekends in New York City and had high expectations that this one would be good, however his friends, mood was becoming a damper.

"Let's not talk business on the weekend, eh?" Tony pleaded; scanning the entrance as several new customers appeared. Two men and women entered and moved towards the bar. Their coats were wet from a light drizzling rain.

"I can't help it!" Bob spat the words out; his anger had not abated since they left work at Global Insurance Company's offices a few blocks away in Water Street, Manhattan.

"We will never finish implementing this godamn system on time!" he reached out and picked up the distinctive brown long-necked bottle and took a mouthful of beer.

Tony turned back to Bob. "Look it's only a job, what the hell's the matter with you anyway?" Impatience crept into his voice.

Bob put his beer down on the bar, hunched up on a tall stool and cupped the bottle in his hands as if warming it. He ignored Tony's question and picked up the "New York Post" and stared at the headlines. The lead story still contained details of the slaughter of the Israeli Olympic Team in Munich."

"September 1972 was not a good month for them!" His thoughts were invaded by the images of the slaughter he had seen in previous newspapers. "Poor Bastards!" he murmured and was momentarily distracted from his own problems.

Tony nudged him, as two more women entered the bar, a smile crept slowly over his face in anticipation. "What about these two?" he questioned. "I'll bet they could take your mind off your troubles," he wagered, hoping Bob's dark mood would dissipate soon.

"Hell! They are too old for me!" Bob looked squarely at Tony whose face had frustration written all over it. He decided to add to his agony. "Forget it Tony, I'd rather go back to work and face Kearsley than those two hags!"

Tony's mouth sagged; the disappointment seemed to deflate him visibly. Bob smiled to himself at Tony's reaction.

"What's wrong with Kearsley? Tony eventually retorted, thankful for a change of subject.

"He's management!" Bob barked and twisted his face. "He's got no idea about standards, conventions or project management for that matter!... Just get it done!" he mimicked his boss, "Just do it! To hell with conventions!" His eyes narrowed just like Kearsley's did when he was under pressure from his staff.

Tony shot a hard look at Bob, then softened; 'You're a fool!" He chuckled and drained his beer, then waved to the bartender for another round.

"I tell you man, if we get this system to work it will be a miracle, it's like the Wild Wild West!" Bob would not let it rest.

"It's Jim's problem, not ours!" Tony was attentive now and could not ignore his friend's rantings. He had been through this several times since they both left "Big Blue" a couple of years ago. They met at IBM four years previously where they had trained as Cobol programmers. Sharing the same sense of humor and the same year of birth they had become firm friends and always worked on the same projects whenever possible. Six months ago, the promise of larger salaries lured them to The Global Insurance Company and they left IBM with mixed feelings. Bob needed money to support his now pregnant girlfriend, Janet Davies, who lived in Newark, New Jersey and Tony needed it to frequent the clubs and bars of Manhattan before his youth slipped away.

"Hell IBM was frustrating but at least it had discipline and conventions!" Bob paid the barman and took a long drink from the distinctive brown colored bottle. "You know I came across at least three conventions for writing year dates last week" he paused, "some were downright frivolous!"

Tony became bored again and his attention returned to the blonde and her girlfriend. Two older men hovered near to them; their expensive suits looked out of place in the dumpy surroundings. The blonde smiled coyly at them and instantly knew where her next drink was coming from.

"Aw shit!" Tony whispered under his breath, he turned squarely and faced Bob. "You know Cobol has no standard for writing dates!"

"Yeah! Yeah! I know, I know! But it sucks, one guy used the word 'time' another used 'date' and another used 'floss!" his face screwed up in a frown. "Godamn it! Floss?" he repeated, "What the hell does that mean?" he asked no one in particular.

"So what?" Tony was tiring of the subject and glanced around the dingy room looking for some feminine distraction. The jukebox belted out the Four Tops, "I'll be there" and Tony's feet moved involuntarily to the driving beat. "I've never seen you so agitated before!" Tony sneered, "What's the real problem?"

Bob rested against the bar leaning on one elbow and looked blankly around. He said, almost to himself, "If this lousy project gets delayed – no bonus, - no bonus, - no abortion – no abortion- no life for yours truly!" Bob looked grim, his jaw clenched firmly closed and his eyes were dark pools of self-pity.

Tony started at him in disbelief, his mouth fell open. "You're…..You're not thinking about an abortion?" he stuttered, "Surely Janet would never go through with it?"

"Look Tony! Janet thinks she's having twins! Godamn twins!" he emphasized. We will never be able to support an instant family!" desperation showed in his eyes momentarily. "I just don't know what to do!" he searched the room blindly for an answer.

"You'll find a way!" Tony said lamely, conviction escaped his intonation.

"If I don't soon, I'll blow this place and try California!" The words hung in the air as if they had carved their own place permanently in the sea of noise, which surrounded them. They both stood silent for a full thirty seconds; the atmosphere was stifling.

"Janet wants to get married and have the kids, she's determined," Bob said at last.

"Why don't you get her to give them up for adoption?" Tony asked uncertainly.

"Once she has seen them, she will never do it,…..Remember she's Irish." Bob took a quick slug of his drink. "If I'm around, her family will just lean on me and we'll all suffer!" He was feeling sorry for himself. "If I'm not around she'll give them up and they'll get a better start in life!" He did not sound convincing even to himself. His eyes were blank as if he had drifted to another place. An awkward silence again isolated them from the bar's noise and Tony felt a sense of outrage building up inside of him.

"Hell, let's enjoy ourselves!" suddenly Bob turned and looked around the room again, he had made a decision, the relief showed in his face. He sat up straighter, as the burden seemingly lifted from his shoulders. "Even those two old hags look good now, let's buy them a drink!"

CHAPTER 1

"Welcome Home Columbia!" were the simple words spoken by Joseph Allen in Mission control as the first reusable spacecraft touched down at Edwards Air Force Base in California.

This historic landing on April 15, nineteen eighty one at 4:21 p.m. EST created the background noise in the grubby office of a small orphanage situated on Liberty Street, Newark, New Jersey. The news momentarily distracted the three adults in the room, who up until then had been lost in their own private thoughts. No one spoke; the old radio's only competition came from outside. Playing in the small yard were two eight-year-old boys with their GI Joe Walkie Talkie sets. They had been given new batteries for their last years Christmas presents and could now use them for the first time.

It was an overcast, gray day in Newark with a light biting wind, making it unusually cold for April, but the boys did not notice it as they called each other on their radio handsets.

"GI Ray!" GI Ray! to GI Base, come in?" Base was in the deepest jungle about twelve feet away from GI Ray, hidden behind an overgrown Rhododendron bush.

Ray's twin brother Jon crackled back "Base here! Base here! Come in" The boys could not hide their excitement at being able at long last to play with their second hand but functional gift for the first time.

In the grim office, an old lady was shuffling the many papers that were associated with the adoption process, while a middle-aged couple, the Bennetts, watched the torturously slow progress. The office was once the living room of a formal mansion built by the wealthy owner of a department store in the center of Newark. Long past its glory days the house had become too expensive to maintain and was donated to the city in nineteen fifty. As in all of these cases the house was difficult to convert and update due to the various building codes, so it progressed through various uses ranging from quarters for the homeless to a drug rehabilitation center, or whatever was the political flavor of the day. Today it was an orphanage with about eighteen resident children ages ranging from five to seventeen years old.

With decades of neglect the place did little to attract visitors. The exterior was a patchwork of cheap repairs designed to keep the weather out and the interior was overrun with decay and could at best be described as dilapidated. Paint had not been applied to the interior for over twenty years and the rising dampness caused the old layers to peel off at various rates of speed revealing a myriad of colors which created a pictorial history of the ages the house had lived through. The windows were opaque to daylight due to the successive layers of dirt, which the environment had relentlessly provided. The building itself seemed to be waiting and wanting to die.

Robert Bennett concentrated hard on the commentator's description of this momentous event. Columbia returning to earth stirred his memory of the Jules Verne novel "*Journey to the Moon*" which predicted such feats over one hundred years ago. His interest heightened as the craft approached landing. His professional instincts took over his consciousness and took him back to his job in Air Traffic control at San Francisco Airport.

Outside the boys were still enjoying their mission in "Deepest Vietnam" locating a target for the imaginary airforce to bomb and frantically calling on walkie-talkies to let each other know where they were.

Ray was the elder twin by one hour and the brighter. He had long blond unkempt hair and lively blue eyes, which absorbed all that they saw. He had an angelic face, and his inquiring nature kept him in trouble because of all the questions he asked about anything and everything. Always with a ready smile Ray was the favorite of the two boys and therefore was afforded more attention by everyone. His current interest was repairing radios usually found dumped alongside the railway line that ran close to the south side of Liberty Street. He would dismantle them then try to reassemble a working model, but rarely was successful. This occupied hours of his time and he learned how and why radios worked which was to stay with him forever. Jon was the quieter brother, almost brooding in nature; and deferred to Ray's lead most of the time. His dark brown hair disguised the fact that he was Ray's twin, although you could tell that they could be related when the boys were together.

Jon had the same blue eyes as Ray's but the brightness was clouded by a glazed look of confusion and anger rooted in such an uncertain start in life. Being the younger brother, Jon seemed less confident, more reserved, and almost reticent to engage in conversations with adults. His distant look and cool nature gave Jon the perception of a loner, and people tended to ignore him in favor of Raymond. He did not resent his brother's popularity, preferring to stay in the background and follow Ray's lead, which currently manifested itself as an acute interest in radios for both of them.

This common interest had brought them even closer together recently.

The boys had now located a target and were calling in for an air strike. "Bravo one! Bravo one!...This is GI Ray bombing coordinates one zero one...repeat...one zero one." Ray mimicked his movie heroes. "Roger. over and out!" Jon was now the pilot.

Inside the orphanage the adoption papers were finally being assembled for signature. It was now close to 5:00 p.m. and the woman was anxious to leave this depressing neighborhood and return to the Marriott Hotel at Newark Airport. Sitting on the edge of the old, grimy wing chair she opened her purse and nervously fingered the three airline tickets to San Francisco, The flight was scheduled for 9:30 a.m. the next morning.

The radio again crackled with the news of Columbia's arrival.

"Captain Robert L. Crippen of the Navy and John W. Young have brought the eighty ton gliding vehicle with its stubby Delta wing, to a smooth landing. This is the first time a space vehicle has returned to earth in such a way so that it can be flown again"

The old lady showed no emotion as she handed the papers to Mr. Bennett, who took them gingerly and sat down to read them. Although familiar with their contents he again scanned them dispassionately while his wife looked anxiously at him with ten years of anticipation in her eyes. Only the radio offered relief from the stifling silence that surrounded the three people. No one ventured to break the somber mood, as if under some kind of spell.

Finally the husband looked up from the papers and asked "Are you still certain that you want to adopt the boy?"

With an imperceptible nod she whispered "Yes". Clutching her purse so tight that her knuckles turned white. She lowered her chin to her chest and her eyes misted over. Nothing had changed her mind throughout the process, she had wanted a son of her own but was unable and now at forty-five she felt a baby would be too much to handle. An eight-year-old son would give some purpose to her unfulfilled life, and she wanted to complete the formalities and leave as soon as possible.

Mr. Bennett quickly signed all copies where marked and handed them back to the old lady brusquely. She separated the papers, put the originals in her file, and handed a copy directly to Mr. Bennett, her eyes contained a mixture of sadness and boredom. No hand of congratulations was offered, no smile volunteered, as this procedure was routine to the old administrator who neither shared the joy nor the apprehension of the moment and had long ago sworn that she would not become emotionally involved with any of the kids.

Mr. Bennett then stood up stiffly, stepped over to his wife, and handing her the envelope with one hand, placed his other under the woman's elbow and gently lifted her up from the torturously uncomfortable chair.

"Where is the boy now?" Mr. Bennett asked quietly, there was an edge to his voice.

"In the yard!" was the dry reply. The old lady turned towards the door and said that she would bring the boy to them. "These were all his belongings!" She pointed to the small tattered suitcase standing in the hall. The couple did not speak, there was no disturbance to the stillness of the room, even the radio fell silent as if to honor the darkness of their decision. This silence was shattered when the large front door slammed shut announcing the return of the old Administrator. Along side her was a fair-haired young boy, his face flushed. He smiled weakly; however, his eyes were filled with apprehension.

"You remember Mr. & Mrs. Bennett don't you Raymond?" the old lady asked flatly without emotion.

"Yes Ma'am," replied the boy hesitantly.

"Well they want you to live with them and have come to take you tonight."

Ray glanced at the suitcase in Mr. Bennett's left hand and panic welled up inside of him, he did not know what to do or what to think, but instinctively felt that something was wrong, his stomach felt tight and his breathing labored. His head was swimming in confusion, was it pleasure or pain to leave this place? He could not tell. His mind would not focus; he was in a slow motion dream as the adults shuffled him to the door. What was happening to him? He was outside now, the cold air blanketed his body, and realization still did not surface from within his distracted mind. He remembered the car doors slamming, the engine starting and the slow ride into the streets of Newark. Something had changed forever but he could not comprehend it.

Jon watched from the cover of the Rhododendron bush, his eyes glistened with anxiety as he tried desperately to hold back the tears.

CHAPTER 2

Flight 44 NEZE Airlines was approaching Auckland, New Zealand at twenty four thousand feet having descended from its cruising altitude of thirty one thousand feet. Captain Douglas Brown glanced at his Tag Heurer Chronometer, it showed 11:51 p.m., December 31, illuminated by the dim cockpit lights.

Originally scheduled to take off from Christchurch on the South Island at 6:30 p.m., the Boeing 737 was delayed due to crew availability. The official reason given was sickness; however, the disappointed passengers knew that like them, few people wanted to miss the biggest party of the millennium, including the flight crew of NEZE 44.

A reserve crew had been scrambled together, and after a four-hour delay the aircraft left the safety of the Earth at 10:24 p.m. and headed northward for the hour and forty-minute journey. This delay now ensured that the passengers and crew would all celebrate the beginning of the new millennium locked together in a flying tube of aluminum, surrounded by forty miles of wire and over one million individual parts, all controlled by sophisticated micro chips and computer systems.

Good fortune, it seemed, had temporarily deserted the crew of four and the thirty-three passengers on board NEZE 44 and to compensate for this, Captain Brown authorized free drinks for all passengers as soon as cruising altitude had been reached. This gesture had little effect on the mood of everyone, but no one refused the offer. Each passenger settled down with their choice of "poison" and quietly reflected on their spoiled plans for this unique eve.

With no other air traffic, Christchurch control vectored Flight 44 on the most direct route to Auckland, New Zealand's largest city. "Flight 44, head zero four zero...repeat zero four zero...acknowledge!" the metallic voice from the control tower waited.

"Confirm... zero four zero," Captain Brown replied and turned the aircraft northeast toward Kaikura. Hidden in the darkness below them was New Zealand's most dramatic coastline, reputed to be the most beautiful in the world. On clear days and at lower altitudes, passengers could see the humpback whales frolicking in the sea, but tonight there was no such diversion.

The two flight attendants moved quietly and efficiently down the ninety-foot long aisle serving the free drinks and snacks to the quarter full plane. Their mood hovered somewhere between disappointment and melancholy; after all, they too were missing out on the celebration of celebrations. Between service runs, they stopped to talk in muted tones at the rear galley telling each other of their hopes and promises for the new millennium.

The third drink seemed only to deepen the gloomy mood as the passengers sat entombed in their own thoughts. The only distraction was the increased cackling of two passengers sitting in the middle of the plane. Like many drunks, they began talking loudly, as if each suspected that the other had suddenly become deaf. Their conversation was sporadically interspersed with raucous laughter in response to some incomprehensible joke.

The rest of the passengers mused that at least two people were happy and making the most of the situation. No one else could summon up the energy to break into the small island of euphoria in the sea of melancholy.

Doug Brown, the pilot was an Australian who had learned to fly with the Australian Royal Air Force over thirty years ago. His eighteen year old marriage to a New Zealand woman was "in the toilet" and he was thankful to be able to take over this flight thus avoiding either another tumultuous night arguing with his wife or on a lonely bar stool in an overcrowded bar.

He loved to fly and did so whenever he could. It was not because he had been ambitious to climb the company ladder that he volunteered for the "unsociable" journeys over holidays, birthdays, and anniversaries, but simply an overwhelming desire to fly. Few people in the world can really experience the feeling of freedom that comes with controlling the gravity-defying act of leaving and returning to Earth. He never thought for one moment that his wife resented his absences and love of flying. She had been wrapped up with the three kids and had her own routine including her friends and interests. It had been years since they had spent any time alone together as she never wanted to leave the home, and he, on the other hand, could not remain earth-bound for long. It never occurred to him that it was not only the kids that kept her home.

Considered ruggedly handsome, Doug's lean body gave the impression that he was taller than six feet that his medical records indicated. Fifty years had taken a toll and the stress of conflict was written all over his wrinkled face. His light blue eyes had heavy lids, and his nose was slightly off center due to a break at the bridge. His clean shaven jaw had a dimple not unlike Kirk Douglas. These worn out looks, however, were deceiving as he kept himself in the prime of fitness and was considered one of the best pilots with New Zealand Air.

He joined New Zealand Airlines ten years ago after retiring from the military, and he and his wife moved back to Christchurch, her hometown.

It was only uneventful flights like this, which triggered these reminiscent thoughts as he mechanically scanned the many dials and lights which, indicated that all was well. His conversation with Bill Scott his younger co-pilot was perfunctory as he seldom let colleagues into his private hell. Bill, broke into his thoughts. "Kaikoura Beacon coming up! Turn zero ten degrees, Doug?" It was more of a question.

"Roger!" Doug replied and turned the 737 northward.

The 737-200 was very responsive designed to fly over two thousand miles with a full payload of one hundred and twenty four passengers making this an easy haul for the Pratt and Whitney engines. Doug liked the 200; it had an unrivalled safety record due to the advanced avionics and an automatic flight control system which provided for automatic approaches in bad weather under category 11 conditions, defined as one hundred foot ceilings and twelve hundred foot forward visibility. "This capability would not be needed tonight," he thought.

The plane turned north past Picton and over Cook Strait, the small stretch of water separating the North and South Islands of New Zealand. Passengers on the port side could see the orange glow of Wellington's lights and speculated about the grand celebration now happening in the capital city. Forty minutes later, they were approaching Auckland, "The City of Sails" and current home to The America's Cup, the ultimate prize for large yacht racing.

Having completed the initial approach to Auckland, Doug began procedures for the final approach. He glanced to his port side, Auckland's Harbor Bridge, outlined by brightly colored lights, was the most prominent landmark. He pinged the attendants' call system twice, the traditional warning to cabin crew to prepare for arrival. At 11:55 p.m. the plane descended through ten thousand feet, the runway lights were now clearly visible to the two pilots. Bill thought aloud, "There should be no delays in landing tonight, there's nothing else in the air, or on the ground, for that matter."

At three thousand feet, the 737 leveled off and approached the airport at one hundred and thirty knots with the undercarriage down and flaps fully extended. Doug glanced at his watch again, 11:59 p.m. He could hear the passengers beginning to count down to the New Year as he focussed on the brightly lit runways.

Land runway one," a hollow voice from the tower instructed, "Repeat, runway one!" The city lights shone like beacons welcoming the new visitors to the party.

"Ten! Nine! Eight! Seven..." the passengers were counting down to the New Year.

"At least we'll go down in history as the first plane to land in the new millennium," Bill muttered as he performed his routine tasks.

Doug's face was contorted in concentration as the winds buffeted the plane slightly. He confirmed to the tower, "Runway one in sight"..

The mood in the Tower was somber, if not slightly agitated, as the lone flight made the final adjustments to its approach path, Colin Walker and his supervisor were not happy about missing out on the celebrations.

Walker glanced at the console clock, "Fifteen seconds before the new millennium," he called over to his supervisor acidly.

He followed the lone blip on the radar denoting the NEZE 44 was about three miles away to the south and turning for the final approach.

He watched the screen intently but his mind wandered to the house party, which he was missing, and the argument he had had with his wife, when he told her he had to work. These thoughts provoked an angry feeling when he imagined his wife alone among the partygoers flirting shamelessly to punish him somehow for not being there. "He'd be there in an hour," he consoled himself.

His eyes passed from the radar screen and back to the digital clock mounted on the console. The red numbers flashed in the New Year, 24:00 0100. The red symbols shone momentarily in the darkness of his retina as the console went blank and he lost contact with NEZE 44. He opened his mouth to speak, but no words came. Seconds later the power to the other buildings died, and darkness washed over the airport. Briefly, the lights tried to flicker back to life as the auxiliary power unit kicked in, but they died again. It was as if a dark blanket had covered Auckland.

"I've lost it...It's gone!" Walker panicked in the darkness.

"What the hell!" Doug cursed as Runway one's lights disappeared into the darkness.

"We've lost contact with the tower!" Bill screamed.

There were no lights save that of the wing lights and no response from the tower. Doug immediately switched to the automatic pilot and reluctantly gave up control to the sophisticated on board computers. The 737 glided downward into the darkness guided by its own sensors giving the pilots time to frantically look for any reference points in the blackness outside.

The digital clock in the cockpit registered in the New Year as the passengers cheered loudly blissfully unaware of the drama unfolding. Suddenly the plane shuddered and lurched downward. Air speed dropped as the engines rapidly reduced their fourteen thousand pounds of thrust. The instruments became useless, and the automatic pilot function ceased to operate. Both pilots were baffled by the loss of power on the ground and in the air. They fought desperately to quell the rising panic that had now invaded the cockpit No amount of training had prepared them for this emergency, but instinctively, Doug banked away from the city desperately trying to control the plane. There was no response to the throttle now and at two thousand feet, the plane spiraled downward into the darkness below.

No one at the airport heard the "MAYDAY" distress calls and there was no radar working which would indicate the plane's fate.

There was only blackness and silence.

CHAPTER 3

The Arctic wind roared across the rugged Uelen landscape searching frantically for any weaknesses that it could exploit and wreak havoc. It swirled violently challenging the very foundations and fabric of any obstacles, both natural and man made, which lay in its path. Millions of large snowflakes were whipped into a blinding frenzy, reducing the visibility to merely inches. The storm's current target was the small hotel that had been battered relentlessly for six hours as the wind raced around the wood and cinderblock structure trying, desperately, to invade the new building.

In contrast to the bleak conditions outside, the warmth of the New Year's Eve party was startling. The log fire crackled in the oversize stone fireplace and supplemented the electric heating system; both sources of heat were more than a match for the storm.

"Boy that storm is something!" Mary Allen shivered as she lifted her glass of Californian champagne and sipped it sparingly. She had no intention of suffering a hangover from this night's festivities.

"Sure is!" her husband growled, "Hope it does not affect our flight tomorrow!" He took another swig of his Canadian club.

"I'm really looking forward to travelling in one of these M1-2 assault helicopters." His tone had a tinge of school boy excitement, "That's what attracted me to the trip in the first place, the flights in the old B-17 and the Russian chopper!"

"Me too!" Frank Holl joined the conversation, "I only hope the pilots will be good!" he added' concern etched into his furrowed brow.

"I'm sure they will be.... If they're sober!" Bob laughed loudly then glanced around at the other eight couples sitting at the adjacent tables, feeling a little conspicuous.

"How long will the trip take?" Sylvia Holl asked, her voice sounded disinterested.

"It's about two hundred miles to Nome, so we may be in the air an hour, maybe an hour and a half!" Bob speculated. "But this storm might prove troublesome!"

Sylvia shivered involuntarily at the mention of the storm.

"Wanna dance?" David L'Costa stood unsteadily next to Mary's chair

"Sure!" Mary stood up slowly and winked at her husband before being dragged onto the dance floor, leaving Bob to carry the conversation with Frank and Sylvia.

Sinatra began singing "My Way." Bob smiled as he watched his wife being pulled and pushed around the small dance floor.

Bob Allen was a burly, red-faced man with thick gray hair, bushy eyebrows, square chin and large mischievous brown eyes. A proud Canadian, he had made his money through timber, working his way up from lumber jack to mill owner. His large scarred hands dwarfed the whiskey bottle as he liberally poured out two drinks. "This storm was not in the forecast, I don't much like it being so isolated."

Frank Holl listened intently to Bob; the frozen north was new to him, as he had lived all his life in California. He had amassed a modest fortune as a Certified Public Accountant and he hated the outdoors. It had been his wife's idea to celebrate the new Millennium in this unique fashion. Frank was slightly built with thinning brown hair. He wore gold rimmed spectacles and had pointed features, his demeanor was nervous, especially at Bob's discomfort about the storm.

"Serge told me that this place has a strange history, " Bob turned to Frank and changed the subject.

"Really! ...It does have a strange feel about it." Frank gazed around the room.

"Yeah! It is a converted barracks! Apparently Uelen was a military and early warning base because it was so close to the U.S.A. That's why it has a small airport. This whole complex was military. When it was abandoned, a local entrepreneur converted it into a rustic resort to attract hunters and fishermen."

"I can see how it would appeal to outdoorsman, real remote, rugged isolation and all that," Frank added unenthusiastically.

"It is known as earth's last unexplored region ... although Captain Cook charted the waters back in the seventeenth century," Bob sipped his whiskey thoughtfully.

"Um ...took its time to develop eh?"

"Yeah, I guess the majority of people are not interested in fifty pound halibut or three thousand pound Kodiak bears!" Bob grinned. "So the Wilderness Lodge chain built a hotel in Nome then converted this as its twin. It had all the utilities left by the military so it was easy." Bob took another sip of whiskey and looked around for Mary. She was on her way back to the table; David had abandoned her for someone else. He stood up to greet her, swaying slightly.

"I hope you can manage the second New Year's eve party in Nome?" she said sternly, it was more like a question, but she did not expect an answer.

"Wouldn't miss it for the world!' He grinned stupidly. "Loved the flight in the old Flying Fortress, it took me back, but I'm really looking forward to the helicopter ride tomorrow. If we fly low enough we might see some whales!"

Geographically Uelen was two hundred miles from Nome Alaska but they were not only separated by the Bering Strait but also by the International Date Line. This mythical line around the Globe meant that Uelen would be one of the first locations to celebrate the New Millennium and Nome would be the one of the last. The Wilderness Lodge chain took advantage of these phenomena and marketed itself as the first and last hotel chain to celebrate the new millennium. The three-day package included flights in rare aircraft and two parties either side of the Date Line and attracted twenty adventurous souls.

Mary shivered and looked at Sylvia Holl. "You cold Sylvia?"

"A little," she was barely audible over the noise.

"Cold!" Bob Allen interrupted Cold! You've got no blood in your veins!" he chuckled.

"It was cold this morning when we arrived! Remember.?" They all cast their minds back twelve hours or so.

The sun shone brightly and disguised the fact that the temperature was minus twenty degrees Celsius, which would register as the highest of the day. Twenty passengers disembarked from the famous Old World War 11 plane, via a small steel stairway and were lead towards the cold bleak air terminal.

After passing through immigration and customs, which involved a circular process of collecting their luggage, having it inspected then finding it again; they carried it outside to the waiting horse-drawn sleighs. The visitors were loaded four persons to a sleigh where they were immediately covered by blankets and bearskins. The huddled together searching for warmth as the fierce cold penetrated the layers of protection.

Bob Allen shivered and rubbed his hands together vigorously, "Cold enough to freeze the...." His wife Mary nudged him hard causing him to leave the sentence unfinished. "Behave yourself," she scolded and raised her eyebrows disapprovingly. She glanced self consciously at the other couple sitting opposite and smiled weakly. "Look at those mountains! They look like a collection of cathedral spires! Aren't they magnificent?" All four passengers turned and marveled at the pristine scene.

The sleighs moved off in procession each drawn by one horse and they covered the five kilometers to town in fifteen minutes. Only the sound of the horse bells invaded the stillness and they provided a warning that the visitors were nearing the hotel. Serge Gorbechov, the hotel manager, stood anxiously on the wooden porch, waiting to greet his guests. He shook hands with each person as they disembarked, a near perfect set of white teeth on display in a permanent smile. He directed them though the double doors and into the lobby of the hotel. The guests milled around the small room, stamping their feet and rubbing their hands to encourage their blood circulation.

They all turned when Serge reentered the hotel and his shrill voice broke the silence.

"Welcome! Welcome!" he beamed again speaking good English accented by his guttural Russian tone. "All your rooms are ready and your keys are in the envelopes on the desk over there," he pointed to a heavy pine table in the corner of the room.

Somewhere in the hotel a clock chimed one p.m. and several guests checked their watches, some adjusted them for the time change.

"Interesting trip!" Chuck Hislop, a ruddy faced American commented, I've been on the road for about ten hours now!"

"It would have been fascinating if it wasn't for the damn cold!" Art Goulet gave a nervous laugh and blew into his cupped hands.

"Yeah I'm not used to this at all." Chuck responded.

"There is hot coffee and tea and of course alcoholic drinks available," Serge interrupted, pointing to the bar to the left. "Please help yourself."

The women moved towards the pine table, and searched for their keys, chattering nervously. Three men walked to the bar and poured a coffee, then added a healthy measure of brandy, the remainder began sorting through their luggage. The hotel lobby emptied slowly.

After unpacking eight visitors ventured out into the small town, the small stores opened especially for them.

"Looks like an old frontier mining town," commented Red Cameron, a compact looking man from Texas who could not get used to the cold.

"Yes, something like the towns that sprung up in the gold rush days!" Bob Allen replied. "Wouldn't surprise me if there wasn't gold here." He added.

"You're probably right!"

At 3.45 the weather closed in and thirty mile per hour gusts whipped the snow into fog-like clouds and the temperature dropped to thirty below. The eight visitors retreated hastily to the comfort of the hotel.

Although relatively small the three-story hotel dominated the town and was surrounded by several smaller stores and a stable. The town had, in fact been modeled off an old American mining town. The only concession to the Twenty-first century was the small section of electric streetlamps and electric power supplied to the half dozen tourist shops and hotel. Two diesel engines courtesy of the Russian Army were located behind the Wilderness Lodge and generated the electric power which provided all the heat and light to the main buildings. These engines were accustomed to working in adverse conditions, and had been renovated in 1996 when sophisticated micro-control panels were installed to monitor performance. Any problems were automatically relayed to a service center five hundred miles away. This center then scheduled a visit by an engineer periodically to repair and maintain the equipment, such a visit occurred only last week.

The cold weather may have curtailed the shopping spree, however it did not interfere with the planned festivities. New Year's Eve Dinner included local fish based soup laced with vodka followed by salmon steaks with potatoes and an ice cream based dessert. Wine imported from California was liberally served, and the ice wine from Canada, where the grapes are picked frozen, was a big hit.

Serge directed the proceedings ably happy to be the master of ceremony on such an auspicious occasion. The restaurant was crowded with some six Russians, twelve Americans and eight Canadians, all talking through an alcoholic haze, not caring if anyone was listening. By 11:30 p.m., the language barriers disappeared along with self-consciousness and singing enveloped the hotel A small space was cleared to facilitate dancing. Frank Sinatra crooned, his famous songs accompanied by at least fifteen other voices, each with different words and different tunes.

"Well the party is in full swing now!" Bob Allen brought them back to the present and looked at his Rolex Oyster. "It's nearly midnight!" He leant over and picked a full bottle of champagne out of an ice bucket and topped up four glasses.

The room was filled with a cacophony of sounds, singing, shouting, and laughter and the dance floor oozed as gyrating people were dragged, spun, pushed and stepped on in a dancing melee. Suddenly the recorded sounds of London's Big Ben filled the room as it struck twelve; in it's own inimitable fashion. Balloons floated from the ceiling and everyone embraced in friendship and hope as the new millennium entered the room. Bob Allen led the singing of "Auld Lang Syne".

Somewhere during the little recognizable second verse, the hotel plunged into darkness; the singing escalated into shouts and screams as total blackness enveloped everyone. Serge scrambled through the crowd towards the kitchen. He blindly felt for the main power switches and flicked them off then on, anticipating a flood of light to replace the unwelcome darkness. Disappointment tinged with fear overcame him. He cursed in Russian and groped his way to the front entrance doors where he was faced, unexpectedly, by the nothingness of blackness. He stared blankly into the void of the blizzard. The streetlights were lost in the night as if some giant had snuffed them out like candles. Not daring to open the doors to the fury outside, he felt the coldness of the storm reach in and embrace him and he shivered involuntarily. It must be his imagination, but the interior temperature seemed to be dropping.

"We have no power," he yelled out, a tinge of panic entered the room. A feeling of danger flooded over him as he sensed rather than saw the nearest street lamp slowly fall towards him. The one thousand-pound pole that was once a stout firtree just caught the base of the entrance doors causing them to crash open just missing him, as he stepped backwards. His slight body was thrown to the floor. He shouted, "Help!" but this was lost in the roar of the wind, which burst into the Hotel.

The five-foot opening caused a wind tunnel of frightening proportions and the restaurant became an extension of the arctic conditions outside. Momentarily confused, the guests were stunned; some women began to scream fruitlessly at the brutal intrusion of the weather.

Led by Bob Allen several guests helped Serge and together they forced the doors shut temporarily. The damage was already done; the temperature inside the hotel was well below freezing point now.

"The opening must be blocked...Get a brace!" Anonymous instructions filled the hotel as half a dozen men fought the fury of the wind with only the entrance doors as a weapon. The cook appeared from the kitchen armed with wood, nails, and a hammer and battled through the melee of people towards the entrance. Russians, Americans, and Canadians fought valiantly against the raw power of nature eventually securing the doors with wooden braces and straps. A table was turned on its side and nailed across the opening giving them some degree of protection.

"They're not weather tight," Serge said in dismay, fear rising inside of him.

"They won't be tonight," Bob retorted hoarsely, out of breath from his efforts.

"What can we do?" Serge was panicking again, looking for leadership.

Nature had won the first round. The room was frigid; women huddled together like sheep, their cocktail dresses provided no protection against the bitter coldness.

"Clothes, get clothes, blankets...anything," another anonymous instruction, floated aimlessly around the room.

It was as if the official had fired a starting pistol at the Olympics in the women's hurdle race. Ten women scattered to their rooms, returning with mounds of woolens. Everyone donned something but the coldness pervaded their very beings, there was no heat to counteract the freezing intrusion of the Arctic. The wind had snuffed out the wood fire and the generators were out of action. The buckled doors still leaked the frigid temperatures from the outside causing the moisture inside to crystallize into frozen lace like patterns on the windows.

Leadership in the form of Bob Allen surfaced. Used to travelling in the Great Bear Lake region of Canada's Northwest Territories, he had experience with similar weather conditions. "Let's move to the kitchen for heat," he ordered. He moved through the crowd towards the kitchen. Someone produced a flashlight. "Can we get heat from the ovens?" Bob asked.

"No, they are electric," Serge replied, he sounded disheartened.

"Any place to hold a fire," he demanded.

"No, only the fire place in the lounge area."

"O.K. get someone to try and re light the fire, not much hope!" he argued to himself.

"Is there a basement"

"No!"

"Is there a radio?"

"Yes in my office!"

"Try and alert someone!"

Bob looked around for inspiration while Serge stared blankly at him. "We'll have to make a small inner shelter within the restaurant area!" He sounded more confident than he was. "We can use the chairs and tables for walls."

"There are spare blankets and sheets in the storeroom and a canvas awning we use in the summer," Serge added enthusiastically as he took a flashlight and made his way to the radio.

"Good", was the non-committal reply.

They moved back out to the restaurant and explained the situation to the others. Several flashlights were now in use and they cast an eerie light on the perplexed and scared faces. Everyone was eager to help. It took their mind off the coldness. Tables were stacked on top of each other against the wall to form the apex of a lean to tent. Rope from the storeroom was tied to the top of the tables and then nailed to the floor forming several "beams". First the canvas was draped over the rope "beams" then the blankets and sheets. Eventually an enclosed area measuring about twenty feet by fourteen feet was erected in the restaurant, enough for thirty people to huddle self consciously together. Each other's body heat would help to warm the tent, and spirits were high as they took a position on the floor flanked by strangers in the darkness. The only light was from the flashlights.

They all settled down to a New Years Eve they'd never forget Serge sat fretful, he had used the radio set to request help but was never certain that anyone heard his call.

CHAPTER 4

The old grandfather clock chimed nine forty-five p.m. as it presided over yet another party at 11 Sea View Road, Bondi Beach, Australia. If it could talk, it would relate that this was no ordinary party the drinking was even more excessive than usual, and the sexual atmosphere overcharged on this, the last day of the millennium. The tall clock was out of place; surrounded by the angular furniture of the sixties, and stood alone and aloof like a guardsman in the corner of the large room. This majestic piece was marred by the irreverent adornment of empty Forsters' beer cans; their famous, blue color littered the chaotic landscape. The atmosphere was thick with blue cigarette smoke, and the quadraphonic speakers of the Sony sound system made every attempt to deafen the generation X's eardrums,

"All you need is love," blasted through the house. The Beatles' song was accompanied by fifty other straining voices. The crowd was noisy and exuberant, excited about the prospects of a new millennium.

The host of this party, Jon David, was concentrating on his own party, in his sparsely furnished bedroom overlooking the sea. In the darkened room with him was a new acquaintance known only as Wendy. Opium perfume permeated the air as she moved inquisitively around the room, drifting casually from object to object, her active green eyes missed nothing. She picked up a photograph and examined it closely.

"Who is this she queried?' putting it down before he could answer.

Jon watched her every move; she was a real poser. Long blonde hair framed a beautiful and mischievous face bronzed by the sun; her mouth was narrow with full lips, which constantly asked questions without expecting answers. Jon's eyes were pure lust as he trailed her, trying hard not to look too obvious in his intentions. His heavy drinking made a sophisticated seduction well out of the question by now, although Wendy was still hoping for some finesse, from this American born gigolo. She roamed the room freely, toying with anything that amused her; she was focussing now on the powerful radio receiver neatly tucked into a converted stereo cabinet. This radio was serious radio, and capable of communicating with anyone in the world, she was still now and Jon jumped at the chance to get close to her.

"I'm a Ham" he joked.

"A what?" she frowned,

"A Ham, an amateur radio enthusiast," he elaborated. "We chat with other Hams all over the world."

Wendy's green eyes glinted playfully, "What does Ham stand for?" A frown crept over her face. Jon moved closer, staring at her breasts, which she thrust towards him temptingly.

"Er...the origin of the nickname has been lost over time and ...er ... some operators still speculate about the meaning, but few agree and even fewer care," he slurred slightly.

Wendy toyed with the dials of the Yaesu. "Go on!" she encouraged, not daring to look at him.

"There are hundreds of thousands, perhaps millions of us all over the world," words were difficult for him to form due to the effects of the beer. "We use H.F...er High Frequency Bands to talk to each other over long distances or VHF and UHF to talk locally," Jon was trying hard to hold her attention now. "We have our own Satellites and digital wireless network" he paused trying to collect his scattered thoughts.

She looked at him blankly, incapable of understanding he had just said.

"I can order a Pizza from anywhere in the world!" he said emphatically, laughing weakly at his own joke. "We can even do it in Morse code," he added.

"What's Morse code?" she queried.

Jon rolled his eyes; his patience was stretched taut

Wendy idly snapped a switch to the on position and the set jumped to life. "OOO, Pretty," she cooed coyly as the dials were illuminated in a soft yellow light, and thin needles twitched in anticipation of action. The digital clock flashed 9:59 p.m. as she turned the frequency dial, sensing that her new companion was closing in on her fast. Jon stumbled over to her, desperately trying to fight off the effects of the alcohol and trying to look in control.

Wendy leaned forward in a provocative way, her back to Jon; she concentrated on the hissing sounds emanating from the radio. Her tight short Gucci dress revealed most of her long brown legs as she bent over the set Jon couldn't take anymore and lunged at her ass with outstretched hands hoping that his legs would follow the lead. She was still turning the frequency dial listening intently for something she could understand as she felt Jon's hands on her hips. His tight Levi jeans straining under the obvious pressure of desire, he began to cover Wendy's back with an alcoholic film of passionate kisses hoping desperately for encouragement. Wendy ignored his intentions and continued to focus on the radio. Jon was tugging at his fly with one hand and trying desperately to keep Wendy from moving with the other. This task, not difficult when sober, was near impossible to him now as his fingers tugged at the rugged zipper on his faded Levi jeans. After what seemed like a lifetime in this laughable position, the jeans relented and Jon felt the release of the zip.

"Eureka," he mumbled absently and turned his full ardor towards Wendy.

She smiled in amusement at his determination and then broke out into laughter when he fell to the floor.

"Mayday... Mayday," filled the room in sharp, piercing bursts of sounds. "Mayday, this is flight..".the sounds disappeared as suddenly as they had arrived The words penetrated Jon's subconscious, deeply disturbing him as he struggled to stand up.

Wendy turned her head and asked innocently, "What does Mayday mean?"

He dragged himself off the floor and leaned against her, his muscular body taut; his mind full of anticipation, but an inner sense made him confused and uncomfortable. "What had he heard on the radio? What had she asked?" The words swam around his brain searching for an answer. Mayday is important somehow but make it go away, he struggled with the dilemma. Rational thought had left him in a disturbing void like being in a room searching for a secret door.

Suddenly he tensed, his mind was alert and scrambled past her for the controls, and he turned the dial methodically, searching the airwaves for those haunting words.

"Someth - something wrong, where was it?"

Wendy stiffened, as she sensed his urgency without realizing the implication. Their hands were both on the frequency dial trying to locate the sound again, she was afraid to look at him now.

"Flight 44" shattered the dark silence once again. "Power lost turning for emergency landing. Mayday" These words hung in the air desperately hunting for a resting-place. Everything was in slow motion now; comprehension was lost in an alcoholic fog. Jon fine tuned the frequency and listened to the dying moments of flight 44, somewhere in the darkness of the night.

The silence was deafening.

He was transfixed; drawing himself up he stood staring intently at the radio set, hoping it was all a dream. This could not be happening; his scrambled thoughts slowly came together like pieces of a jigsaw puzzle and were painting a horrible misty picture on which he did not want to focus. Wendy turned and stared at Jon with a whimsical look of incomprehension. She half thought that this was a radio play with some dramatic ending to a half-hour show somewhere in the world. She never for one moment considered it to be real and was confused by Jon's changed attitude. Clearly his ardor was gone, but his inanimate posture in front of the silent radio set was both bewildering and frightening to her.

Slowly Jon reached for the frequency dial and started to turn it trying to resurrect the sounds still echoing in his mind. Time seemed to stand still as he struggled with the reality of the situation. The radio gave no help either, fluctuating between silence and a hissing sound as frequency bands were gently caressed.

No answers lay in this black box of electronics, dials, and levers.

"How could mankind invent such a useless piece of equipment which leaves one knowledgeable yet powerless at the same time?" Jon ruminated.

Seconds rolled into minutes as the couple struggled with their thoughts. Neither one wanted to break the uneasy silence within the room, but both wanted to escape from the situation. Slowly the party sounds began to invade their thoughts as they fought to return back to the reality they knew prior to the dramatic intrusion of flight 44.

Suddenly noise and light burst into the room as a drunken couple fell through the now gaping open doorway. The Beatles invaded the room with, "She loves you yea, yea, yea." The noise was deafening and unwelcome. In contrast to the mood, Jon could not bear this unwelcome intrusion.

The strangers staggered a few more steps into the room before swaying to a halt, as they recognized that the room was occupied. They giggled some poor excuses for an apology and backed out leaving Jon and Wendy in a disturbed silence. The door was still open and Wendy edged slowly over to close it, relieved that she could do something. Jon's mood had decidedly changed for the worse; his demeanor was becoming somber, his eyes became blackened windows to his thoughts and he verged on depression. The atmosphere had become highly charged and Wendy needed desperately to get out of this now claustrophobic room.

Grasping the door handle, she said something about going to the powder room, but Jon did not register anything. Closing the door as she left, she sighed in relief as the barrier between them severed the dark mood. Jon stared at nothing in particular straining to comprehend the last few minutes. The affects of the alcohol were beginning to dissipate and rationality seemed to be within reach if he could only concentrate.

Unconsciously he dialed a frequency on the radio that he was familiar with and started calling the code name of a contact in New Caledonia whom he had known for years.

The metallic voice of Tom Ricer's answering machine requested Jon to leave a message.

CHAPTER 5

Tom Ricer's parents would not recognize his name; he had changed it when he changed his life, years ago. Tom was not a superstitious man; he had been through too much to fear the unknown, but this change of the millennium brought a bad feeling, a feeling he could not shake. Even his annual New Years Eve party on his small farm near Noumae, New Caledonia, could not shake his mood. but this celebration seemed different somehow. These muddled thoughts were interspersed with memories of his early life in the U.S.A. Thoughts, which made his eyes, glisten unexpectedly.

New Caledonia was the larger Island of a small group lying about eleven hundred miles North East of Australia. Its capital, Noumae, situated near the southern tip of this three hundred by twenty five mile strip of land and was home to a misplaced ex U.S. Navy Rating called Tom Ricer. The 'ex' was not the official term used by the U.S. military, as his official discharge had yet to occur. Like many others, the Vietnam War took its toll on Tom and he relocated to a better mental climate in the early 1970's, changing his name along the way.

Tom's HAM code name was "Road Runner" chosen deliberately by him to reflect his choice many years ago. He had been a signalman in the navy, so operating the radio was second nature to him, and he always had his equipment switched on. Although the original radio equipment was rooted in the 70's Tom had updated the equipment regularly and had included automatic signal scanning and recording so that he could sample constantly the frequently used wave bands. This scanning equipment was preset to pick up relatively strong signals as it skipped through the high frequencies, much like sophisticated car radios. Once a message had been identified a recorder, limited to forty-five seconds, was automatically triggered, and this gave Road Runner a flavor of airwaves activity for any given period. This recording capability was also triggered for any incoming calls specifically for him just like any telephone answering system.

Tom listened to the radio daily, if not hourly, it was a habit for him. Tom was a large, burly man. His curly black hair, typical of his black heritage, had been receding for some years now, but he always cut it military short. The gray flecks betrayed his age, estimated to be fifty plus.

He was born to a gentle couple in Georgia, who worked on a small plantation near Dickey in Calhoun County. Although the working conditions on the plantation were relatively good it still was hard work and his parents, Bill and Miriam Robson, always looked worn out and older than their years. His father desperately wanted a better life for his son, but did not have the means to provide it, so Tom worked the plantation as soon as he was able. His chores kept him out of school much of the time, which he did not mind, although it disturbed his parents greatly.

By the time he was 16, he was 190 lbs. His 6-ft. frame was muscular with no excess fat, he looked much like his father and older than his years. Tom enjoyed working alongside his father in the fields and tried to take the lion's share of the heavy work lifting the tobacco bales and digging ditches.

Scratching a living consumed the family's life and left them with little time for play; however, in whatever spare time the father and son could get, they used it to wrestle in front of their small wood framed home. Over the years Tom's father found it more and more difficult to better his son and now only fought defensively in order to conserve his energy, which seemed to drain from him easily now.

"You gittin' too old Pop," Tom would josh when his father lay breathless.

His mother was both proud and apprehensive about Tom. Proud of his size and physique but apprehensive about his gentle nature and how the world might take advantage of it. With little education and no experience in the world, she worried constantly about his future. Bill often suggested to her that Tom should join the Army when he was eighteen, but Miriam resolutely refused to consider this and pushed the idea aside every time he brought it up. This did not deter Bill, and he would tell Tom stories about his friends who had joined the forces; all of them had favorable slants and all of them were untrue.

Life was mundane for the Robsons although they did not recognize it; their simple pleasures of walking, talking and eating had a timeless effect and made one-year roll into another uneventfully. Routine was a way of life for the Robsons and they were comforted by it; however, this was disturbed one evening as father and son strolled down an old cart track together on a balmy summer evening. The moon cast an eerie blue light tinged with the orange of the setting sun as it disappeared over the horizon, a slight breeze rustled the trees.

"He became top sergeant in the Marines." Bill turned to Tom smiling. Tom listened intently suspecting that his father's memory was not always accurate now but nevertheless enjoying the stories.

"Fine figure of a man respected by all, could fight any three people and win," Bill paused, looking skyward and marveling at the sunset and peacefulness of the evening.

Muffled screams pierced the stillness, interrupting his train of thought and Tom felt the hair on his neck rise involuntarily. A sense of danger flooded over them, the elder man felt sickly. Both men slowed, their senses straining to understand the disturbance. They crept forward, hunched down to avoid being seen, by something or someone unknown. After covering thirty yards they saw the taillights of a 1950 dark colored Chevy pick-up, peaking out of the long grass.

"Quiet now" Bill whispered as he haunched lower. Both the men's nerves were taut and their mouths were dry as they moved toward the vehicle. They were close enough now to hear the fretful sob of a woman and immediately crouched low against the truck slowly moving down each side until they reached the cab doors. The scene unfolded itself like some grotesque movie. In the headlights were two white boys about nineteen years old and one black woman entangled in a mess of human depravity.

Bill's anger welled up uncontrollably and he rasped, "You boys in trouble!" He moved to the front of the truck.

The startled boys jumped. "What the shit you doing here?"

The taller boy cursed and ran towards Bill, covering the five yards unexpectedly fast, The girl screamed and was immediately punched unconscious with one blow to the jaw.

Bill hesitated for just a second. The first boy rushed him, pinning him against the truck hood flailing at him with his fists and feet. He kicked Bill sharply on the shin then drove his knee into his solar plexus. Stunned, Bill gasped in pain and as he grasped for his stomach. The second youth now joined in the melee punching Bill's unprotected face continuously.

The speed of events caught Tom unprepared and he watched in horror as his father fell under the lightning quick onslaught. He moved toward the fight quietly and purposefully. The smaller redneck was taken unawares as Tom picked him up in a half Nelson and crashed his head against the hood of the truck. The boy's brief struggle ended instantly and he became a dead weight, his legs buckled beneath him and he slid down to the ground. Tom turned to the taller boy who was still punching a red mass of skin and blood that was his father's face. He had never lost his temper before but something snapped. He moved behind the youth and clamped his hefty forearm around the assailant's neck; his right hand grabbed a handful of hair. The boy screamed in agony and cursed him.

"You're dead man...you're dead."

Arching his back, Tom pulled backward slowly dragging the redneck off his father. The boy kicked him in the shin causing him to misstep, and he fell backwards with his arm still in the strangle hold. Tom fell, pulling the redneck with him. As he hit the ground he heard a sickening crack and felt the redneck land on top of him. Winded by the fall, he lay still fearing that the youth would recover before him. Time seemed to stand still as he stared at the moon through pain filled eyes. Seconds grew into minutes; the only thing that disturbed the stillness was the sounds of someone soon to leave life behind. Adrenaline surged into Tom's arms when the images of his father re-entered his consciousness. He threw the redneck off of him easily and lifted himself to one knee. He stared at the scene in disbelief, to his left the girl lay unmoving on her back with her clothes ripped from her, blood trickling from her mouth. To her right just in front of the truck, the first white boy lay still, face down in the dirt. Beside this boy his father was in a sitting position, his back against the fender and his legs crumpled up beneath him. His head was slumped forward and blood streamed from his face. To his immediate right the other, taller boy, lay on his side, his head in an unnatural position.

Tom staggered over to his father and carefully lifted his head, the torn flesh looked macabre in the eerie shadows cast by the headlights. This movement brought a gasp of pain from Bill whose consciousness was emerging with excruciating pain. Tom looked around for something to wipe the blood from his father's face. He picked up a piece of the girl's dress and dabbed the old man's face gently, then held it to stop the bleeding. Bill slowly regained the use of his limbs and groaned as the pain stabbed at his old body like a thousand red-hot pins.

"You OK Pop?" Tom's voice was dry and full of concern.

The older man nodded and whispered dryly, "I'll be alright in a minute."

Tom straightened up and looked over the old Chevy; he walked to the back and pulled out an old blanket. He walked over to the girl and knelt down placing his ear close to her mouth. He could both hear and feel her shallow breathing and he placed the blanket over her naked body.

He heard his father groaning and went over to wipe the blood from his cuts again, his nose had been broken and he had bitten his tongue. "Don't move Pop...Hold this against your nose." Tom then went to the redneck at the front of the truck, he gently rolled him over and cringed when he saw the mash of flesh and bone that once was his forehead. He was not breathing.

"Oh God," Tom exhaled in shock.

The second redneck was in the same condition, his neck broken in the fall. Tom felt the bile in the back of his throat as the realization dawned on him how his life had changed in five short minutes. He fell to his knees and was violently sick, his head spun wildly and dizziness overcame him.

The whimpering from the girl brought him back to reality. He turned and watched as she rolled her head from side to side in tormented agony as she began to regain consciousness.

Tom ignored her and moved over to his father again, he grimaced at the sight of raw flesh, but was thankful his father was beginning to function again. Bill looked up and slowly drank in the horrific scene. He knew without asking the seriousness of what had happened and began to pull himself to his feet. Tom helped him and when he was upright Bill used the pickup to steady himself. His strength was slowly returning and with it his reasoning.

"Those guys dead?" he gasped.

"I, I think so," Tom was barely audible, he felt the bile rise again and he gagged.

"How about the girl?"

"She's alive," Tom rasped.

Bill thought for a full minute swaying on unsteady legs. "Grab those boys and put them into the cab of the truck" he instructed suddenly.

Tom dragged the bodies to the truck and hoisted them into a sitting position on the worn bench seat.

"Turn off the lights," Bill grimaced as pain flooded over him, "and drag the girl off to the side…gentle now."

"Now take the brake off." Bill was moving unsteadily to the rear of the truck.

Tom completed his dad's instructions and followed him to the rear of the truck.

"There's a little ditch about twenty feet ahead, lets roll this crap over to it." The truck was easy for the two big men to push and in a few minutes it rolled into a ditch about five feet deep. The bodies lurched forward smashing their heads against the windshield leaving blood smeared all over the cab.

Tom staggered back to the girl who was drifting in and out of consciousness, wrapped her up in the blanket and picked her up in his arms easily. No one spoke as they moved cautiously through the darkness toward the small cabin they called home. Miriam was distraught when she saw the state of her husband's face. She hugged him tenderly burying her head in his chest; her tears mixed with the blood. She looked at the girl who was bruised and bleeding but overall her condition was less serious than Bill's.

"Tom you tend to the girl," Miriam instructed as she gently worked on Bill's face, which now had swollen in a grotesque manner making him look surreal in the flickering candlelight. Miriam finished cleaning bill up and turned her attention to the girl, tears misted her eyes constantly.

An hour later, the Robsons were sitting around an old neglected dining table, drinking coffee. They all glanced at the girl as she lay whimpering in Tom's bunk. The same thoughts crossed their minds...." This girl had changed their lives forever." There would be no sleep for them tonight; plans had to be made. Bill silently gathered everything of value that he could find in the cabin and wrapped fifty-six dollars, an old gold watch, and Miriam's gold wedding ring in an old scarf. He sat across from Miriam and Tom with tears in his eyes.

"There's a railway line about twenty miles east of here," he paused, his voice failing him. "You have to take a north bound train and get to Atlanta," the tears flowed freely now. "Go to the nearest military office and join up," his voice was thick and had a tone of finality to it, no one argued. Miriam sobbed uncontrollably. "It's the only way!" Bill moved closer to his wife and comforted her. He turned to Tom, "We'll wait until dawn and you have to head always for the sun." At 4 a.m. Miriam held her son for the last time. Bill embraced him tenderly before Tom moved silently out of the house and waved goodbye to the only life he had ever known. He moved eastward, always keeping the sun in his eyes until he crossed the railway line, just after noon.

Two days later, Tom walked into a navy recruiting office, he was dirty, tired, and his brown eyes misty with fear and sadness, but the Petty Officer on duty recognized a prime recruit when he saw one. The Vietnam War was in full swing making the selection process less than selective; thus, Tom was signed up immediately. Immediate arrangements were made for him to be transported to San Diego Naval Base for basic training. This trip in itself proved traumatic for Tom who had never been outside of Calhoun County until now. He missed trains and spent hours waiting around stations depending on friendly faces to guide him; his money ran out two days before he reached the Naval Base, looking gaunt, dirty and more than a little scared.

Twelve weeks of boot camp did not improve his life at all. Like all basic training facilities in the military, authority was often abused, the strong preyed on the weak and the gangs persecuted the loners. It was brutal and made no sense to him; he was totally unprepared for this strange new world. His six-year hitch now seemed impossible to survive and his thoughts constantly drifted back home, his only comfort was the old watch his father had given him.

He had little education and few skills to speak of so Tom's options for advanced training were nil, he found himself limited to performing menial tasks for anyone and everyone. He was bottom of the totem pole of life, and he needed all the courage he could summon to survive the endless challenges the world threw at him. This mundane life continued for eight months until he was assigned to a small supply ship, the U.S.S. Marcy, operating in the South China Sea. Tom was unsure if this was good or bad, but welcomed a chance to escape the brutality and boredom of the barracks.

Launched in 1945, the Marcy was a twenty-thousand ton freighter built for World War II, commissioning, however, did not occur until the commencement of the Korean War where she served as a supply ship in that bitter conflict. Her Navy life was extended when she was refitted for the Vietnam War in 1968. It had a crew of one hundred and seventy and shuttled between the Subic Bay supply base in the Philippines to the war zone off the east Vietnam coastline and Saigon.

The first part of his journey was a two-hour truck ridge to Los Angeles with five other ratings, one of whom he knew, Juan Suarez. He sat quietly, lost in his own thoughts, as the Navy truck made its way laboriously up Route 5 to LAX International Airport. His face was gray with apprehension and his mouth was dry, he remained separate from the others as they laughed and joked and sang along with the Mama's and Papa's "California Dreamin" which belted out from a beat up Emerson radio.

A news bulletin interrupted the music "Walking on the moon was very comfortable." The voice of Neil Armstrong sounded tinny through the small radio speaker.

"Man, that's what I want to be," joshed Ernie Watson, a recent recruit from Tennessee interrupted the interview.

The five passengers turned towards him, "Why?"

Those chicks man, livin' fancy just because of a few days trip in space…It ain't fair. Hell I'd be more famous than Elvis." He smiled broadly.

The others grunted in agreement.

Tom sat alone and reflected about his parents, his home and his future and ignored the lighthearted banter, which merely disguised the other men's fears and apprehensions. He did not know what to expect from his first flight and the unknown was an increasingly worrisome thing for him.

Juan Suarez sensed Tom's mood and casually whispered, "Tom…just do what I do at LAX." Tom smiled a warm smile, but his eyes revealed the fear that was gnawing away at this insides. He never left Suarez's side.

The flight to Honolulu was uneventfully long and Tom even found himself napping during the eight hours in the air. The five men were all transported from Honolulu airport to Hickman Air

Force Base where they were separated to find their own destinies. Tom had to wait four hours for a transport plane to take him to Subic Bay. 30 infantrymen out of Schofield Barracks joined him and his worst fears became true. This trip with army personnel seemed interminable, as he became the brunt of the grunts' entertainment, making him wonder if the army was on the same side as the navy.

"Hey man how big are the oars to row them ships," a large white sergeant began to tease.

"They don't use oars, they use their big hands and feet...HA!HA!HA!HA!" a corporal joined in.

He survived this flight by either sleeping or pretending to sleep. Life indeed seemed to have thrown him another curve ball.

The aircraft landed in Subic Bay at midnight. Tom waited until the grunts had disembarked before he left the plane, then found a place to wait for his transport to the dock area to pickup the ship. A Navy truck appeared at 6:15 a.m. and he threw his duffel bag into the back and climbed in. A beaming face with perfect white teeth introduced himself as Barry Taylor

"You joining the Marcy?" he asked.

"Yeah!" Tom smiled

Both men shook hands. Tom relaxed for the first time this trip and he never felt the half-hour trip to the quayside where the Marcy was moored.

"Permission to come on board, Sir," Barry Taylor addressed the officer on deck.

"Permission granted," the officer responded boredom written all over his face. Both Tom and Barry showed the duty officer their orders as they boarded the ship. He checked their orders against his master list and directed them to their quarters. Barry went forward and Tom aft. He felt lonely again as he moved among the crew without acknowledgement, leaving him feeling as isolated as ever. He stowed his duffel bag on the small bunk allocated to him deep within the ship bowels; deserted by natural light the quarters were cramped and depressing. Tom's eyes misted over.

"Good morning," a young looking petty officer greeted him cheerfully, as he approached.

"Get your kit stowed and I'll take you to the galley."

Tom rubbed his eyes and followed him quietly, disheartened by his new surroundings and already missing San Diego. He only played with his breakfast, his stomach was too unsettled to eat but he managed to drain two mugs of coffee after which he was put to work cleaning up the galley. He merged into the relaxed atmosphere and slowly began to realize that his fears were unfounded. Some kind of normality returned to his life until orders came to put to sea .The crew became edgy, the relaxed atmosphere changed to one of agitation and tension. On the first day out he found himself in sick bay alongside Barry who was also fighting to find his sea legs.

"Man this is bad, I'm dying," Barry was gray. "Tom how do you feel?" he inquired looking up to see Tom vomiting again. A couple of days later they both left sick bay somewhat unsteadily but relieved that the initiating experience was over with the help of Dramamine. This painful experience cemented his friendship with Barry and Tom visited him, in the radio room, whenever he could, picking up some of the jargon and techniques of a radio operator, life began to improve. The crew absorbed the two new crewmen as if by osmosis, there was no single point of acceptance just a gradual inclusion into the small and cramped community life. Tom eventually became relief radioman, which excused him of some of his kitchen duties.

The Marcy shuttled supplies wherever they were required and was always on the move, sailing between Manila, Saigon, Singapore and Jakarta. Tom became comforted by the ship's routine, and began to think of it as a second home, preferring now to be at sea than in port. The shore leaves at Saigon were depressing for Tom as he never related to the country or understood the reason for the war. Tales of atrocities by both sides brought back bitter memories and made him think about his parents more and more. His desire to escape the whole thing became uppermost in his thoughts. Depression slowly consumed Tom, but no one realized it. His soul darkened and morale plummeted, but his quiet nature disguised his black moods. Even the distraction of operating the radio failed to elevate his spirits. The comforting routine had made time meaningless and he could see no end to the conflict both in the outside world and within himself.

In the summer of nineteen seventy-two the murderous monotony was broken when the Marcy was sent to Jakarta to transport some special equipment and observers to Saigon. Prior to leaving Captain Anderson gave most of the crew twelve hours shore leave, to boost morale and break the stifling mood that had embraced the small ship. Barry managed to persuade Tom to go ashore and together with one hundred and twenty white and blue uniforms they hit the local nightlife hard. Traveling in groups of between two and ten men, the sailors scoured the city for excitement, sex, and drink and found them all. At the last bar, The Blue Moon, a fight broke out over nothing important, and remnants of the Marcy crew scattered into the darkness. Tom took a wrong turn, and found himself alone in a dark alley, cornered by three boozed up local thugs who took a dislike to the white uniform and what it represented.

There was a deathly stillness as the three men encircled Tom; he backed further away into the darkened alley - his first mistake. His second mistake was not fighting back, memories welled up inside him and he feared another killing on his hands. The assailants cursed and spat at him, as they assaulted him unmercifully.

"You asshole Yankee, you got no right here!" they screamed, each encouraged by the others frenzy.

Tom crashed to the ground after being kicked in the groin.

"You piece of shit, get out of here," their vocabulary was very limited

Tom curled up in a ball trying to protect himself. He felt little pain after the first minute; unconsciousness anesthetized him from the brutal beating. They stripped him of everything, even his father's watch, and left him to die in the growing pool of blood flowing from his head.

Three days later he woke up in the house of an old prostitute. The stale smell of body odor mixed with cheap perfume was nauseating to him and he fought the urge to throw up. Pain tortured every part of his body, but the real fear he felt was the complete loss of his memory. The woman sat in an old chair watching him intently. Her face had the look of worldliness verging towards world-weariness. Her demeanor suggested she had seen a lot and regretted much.

She had found him staggering blindly around the alleys and guided him to her home. Her search for money disappointed her and when Tom lapsed into unconsciousness she could not move him so let him remain. Tom gradually recovered from his physical beating but his mental health was bad.

With his past now unknown to him and his future unclear, he settled for life with a stranger, frequently protecting her from her clients and herself. The money she earned paid for alcohol to help them dull the pain of living. Tom's muscular body deteriorated rapidly. He suffered constant headaches and now had pain when he peed. Neglect and depravation took its toll and he was at an all time low.

While scavenging around the docks one evening, he came across an old World War II freighter named Kingfisher. A flicker of memory flashed across his mind and he was drawn to the activity. Large wooden crates were being loaded and he noted the words "Farming Equipment." marked on the side of each box. He stood in silence, blankly staring at the activity, The flashes increased and pictures of the Marcy entered his consciousness. He heard a metallic snapping noise and panicked yells flooded the air

Somewhere above him a voice boomed, "Watch out below…"

Tom instinctively threw himself to the ground and heard the sound of wood and metal crashing onto the concrete quay. He looked up slowly, a mixture of curiosity and resentment crept over his face. The Kingfisher's crew scrambled to cover the contents of the crate with tarps. They were too slow and he saw M16 rifles, mixed with splintered wood, strewn all over the Quay. Tom dragged himself to his feet unsteadily, drew a deep breath as he stretched and rubbed his bruised legs. The ships mate approached him menacingly.

"Cover that shit up." He barked at the crew, but his eyes never left Tom.

Tom knew trouble when he saw it and held up his arms gesturing surrender. "Seen nothing, heard nothing," he muttered staring the mate straight in the eye. The guy shot him a hard look then glanced at the crew cleaning up.

"Looking for work," he spat the words out at Tom.

"Could be," Tom rasped, his mouth dry, he needed a drink badly.

"Come on board," the mate smiled a false smile. "Let's have a drink."

"What the hell," Tom muttered to himself. He had nothing to lose; even his life was worthless.

Tom followed the guy up on the Kingfisher's gangplank, and into a small cabin where he was offered a large glass of rum. He drained it immediately and was given another. He was still on board when the mooring lines were cast off and the ship moved slowly out to sea. He spent the next three years shipping contraband wherever and whenever it was wanted.

In 1988, an older and wiser Tom Ricer reached the shores of New Caledonia. He was getting slow and tired and desperately wanted back the stability he knew as a child. His criminal period had rewarded him well and he decided to 'retire 'once again. He landed in Noumae respectably well off, and put a down payment on a small farm and began farming again. His thoughts continually drifted back to Georgia, to his parents and he longed for family life. He was successful and eventually settled down and married a widow with three children. His life had taken a turn for the better and he became a valued member of local society. No one ever knew when he regained his memory, not even Tom, he spoke little of his past. The only intrusion he allowed into his new world was via a H.F. radio set.

In his new life Tom always held a New Years Eve party, inviting many of his neighbors, the eve of the new millenium was no different and the party was in full swing. He normally did not take center stage, but tonight he slurred an appropriate toast allowing himself to think about his parents. As he finished his drink, tears filled his eyes and he left the room quietly to compose himself. He walked into his study and wiped his eyes, he cast a glance around the room and noticed a flashing light on his radio.

It was 12:16 a.m. when Tom's set picked up the call from Sydney. The recording captured the distracted voice of Jon stammering about some crashed aircraft. Jon's voice trailed away and the recorder reset itself for the next message. Tom replayed the message then returned to his party, emotionally composed but distracted by Jon's message.

An hour later Tom idly pressed the play button of the radio recorder whilst nursing a well-needed mug of coffee and two painkillers as the millennium's first hangover slowly enveloped him. The recorder began to spit out the messages in sequence and since it was New Year's Eve Jon's ramblings were the first sounds on the machine. Puzzled by the message, Tom stared mindlessly at the radio, slowly sipping the hot coffee. He replayed Jon's message then pressed the recording scan and listened for any mention of a missing aircraft around 12:00 a.m. He rewound the recording and replayed the tape from 11:50 to 12:10 a.m., but the only message received was the confirmation of a ninety-nine million dollar transfer of funds to a/c # 153-4768-9797. Tom thought nothing about this message. He let the recording ramble on while his mind drifted back to last night and the wonderful time he had had with family and friends. He was lost in these thoughts when his subconscious caught up with some urgent message somewhere at sea.

"Ship drifting in heavy seas, longitude 171, degrees 14, latitude 24, degrees 37, critical condition, no power, close to Minerva reefs."

Tom listened to the message again, his natural instincts bristling while looking at the world map above his radio equipment. The message was timed at 12:15 a.m. and he stared at the map unseeingly the one reminder of his life outside this island that had become his home. Tom had not thought much about Jon's message regarding an aircraft in trouble, but felt ill at ease about the floundering ship.

Still deep in thought he called Jon, not caring that he was in a different time zone.

"He'll still be partying," he thought, mischievously.

"Calling Midnight Cowboy! Midnight Cowboy! Road Runner here," Tom was always amused by the handles chosen by radio HAMs, the names invariably meant something, some innermost secret. Jon's "Midnight Cowboy" handle was a throwback to the hit movie, which had made a big impression on him when he was a boy.

59

After several attempts at raising Jon, Tom was about to give up when a groggy voice spluttered through the speaker of the Japanese made set. Tom could hardly recognize the raspy voice at the other end of the airwaves. Jon sounded hoarse as the thick coating on his tongue turned his American/Australian twang into some less comprehensive babble.

"What the hell are you calling at this time for?" Jon yelled down the microphone, far from the usual retort of Midnight Cowboy. "Have you bastards no sense of time? It's way after midnight here." Tom hesitated in his reply, not sure now if this was all a cruel joke.

"You called me remember," Tom had an edge to his voice.

Jon tried desperately to clear his mind and clear his throat of sand like dryness. He grabbed a half-empty beer can and drained the flat beer in one gulp. His mind was clearer now, but not much. He readjusted his attitude before speaking to Tom again.

"How're they hanging?" He offered to diffuse the moment.

Tom smiled to himself and retorted that they'd seen better days and seem to be hanging so low that they were in danger of becoming detachable. At this they both laughed, the awkward moment gone.

"Been scanning my recordings for a downed plane, but nothing there" continued Tom "at least in that time window. Nothing on the local news either."

Jon groaned "I must be losing it," he drawled. The drink had taken its toll; his head began to pound like hell.

Tom wasn't interested in this self-analysis and broke in "But I did come across an emergency at sea about the same time, maybe that's what you heard."

"No the words were Flight 44. Sounds funny to me, but who knows, I wonder if they both happened in the same area?"

"A new Bermuda triangle," mused Tom.

"We're probably reading too much into it and anyway nothing is confirmed," he continued.

Jon was lost in thought. The downing of the aircraft had profoundly affected him because that is how his parents had died, or so he had been told. He could not escape the feeling that something was amiss.

Tom's voice interrupted him again "I'll check on this ship again, try to find out frequency and location." "Call you back if I find out anything."

Jon signed off and returned to bed, but could not find the comfort of sleep. The news of a floundering ship reminded him of an old, dear friend. His thoughts returned to his childhood and to Sam Walsh, an old retired Merchant Seaman who had befriended him.

"Sam must be well into his 60's by now! Wonder if he was still alive?"

It was Sam that introduced him to he world of amateur radio and to adventure in far away countries. It was Sam who had made his life better and for some reason, it was Sam who now prevented him from sleep.

CHAPTER 6

Tom was still at his radio scanning the H.F. bands for any messages involving ships, but located very little activity at all on the airways. Bored now with his attempts, he glanced at the wall clock, it showed 2:45 a.m., January 1. He switched to the VHF bands to pick up local police.

"Emergency vehicles required at Rue Canq and Eiffel, multiple car accidents!" A harried voice requested.

"What do you expect on New Year's Eve," he thought.

The reports added that there were numerous failures of traffic lights and reduced street lighting, which alarmed Tom, but it was well known that the power supply in the Hebrides was notoriously unreliable. Tom smiled at the last item,

"People are trapped in elevators in several city hotels."

This invoked a humorous image, but he dismissed the subject summarily. He broadened his horizons and searched for the commercial frequencies.

"This is Joe McIntyre reporting again for CNN in Tokyo! The millennium festivities are in full swing," the announcer continued, however, he warned "There is a temporary interruption of trains into and out of Tokyo due, apparently, to power failure. People are advised to avoid public transport," he warned. "More news would follow!".

Tom went to the kitchen for a cup of coffee, "Strange goings on," he thought and remembered his feeling of discomfort at the beginning of the evening. When he returned the reporter was repeating the latest again.

"People are trapped in darkness on these trains, which seemed to splutter to a halt! Most people remained on the stalled trains and pencils of light could be seen as passengers used any emergency flashlights that were available. A few people had exited the trains and made towards nearby stations for safety.

Emergency services were mobilized but these were skeleton crews due to the New Year's Eve celebrations."

The announcer hesitated then began again, "Despite these anxious conditions no panic was reported, although some people were injured jumping from the trains, but nothing serious had been reported."

Tom listened intently. Somehow he thought that this news item was related to the other incidents but he could not rationalize why. He glanced at the clock and it showed 2:50 a.m. in New Caledonia, which meant it was 12.50 a.m. in Tokyo.

The announcer went on to say, "After ten minutes of this stoppage, no reason could be found; all options are still being investigated, including sabotage". He paused for effect. "Those who had flashlights lead others from the trains, Pied Piper like towards the darkened stations where emergency services were on hand to help the aged and injured. It was reported that at one station a lone Scottish bagpiper played Amazing Grace underneath the big clock which remained stubbornly on 12:01 a.m."

Tom's thoughts were distracted by the last comment. It's strange how one country namely Scotland is always associated with New Year's Eve. The bagpipes and Auld Lang-Syne are synonymous with December 31st," his mind wandered.

"Police activity throughout Tokyo is frantic at the notion of sabotage" the announcer repeated again .Tom was startled by the radio.

"The situation has been compared to the 1995 subway gas attack by an extremist group, which claimed several lives," the radio continued.

In Japan the notion of sabotage was not a logical conclusion to any railroad official but no other rational explanation could be found in the early moments of the crisis. The breakdown of the train system seemed so complete as to rule out normal problems. Weather was not a factor with temperatures in the normal range during this time of year, if anything, they were slightly milder than normal. Heavy snow had been limited to the northern mountainous region. Newsmen chased after government and railroad officials for comments about the breakdown. When none were available, they hypothesized about rumors of terrorist activities.

"Riot police are now on alert," one newscaster reported, but qualified the statement as a rumor.

The news agencies concentrated on the feeding frenzy that Tokyo had become each speculating about the breakdown more wildly than the next and scrambling for eyewitnesses to verify their theories. Railway engineers were tracked down and questioned without conclusion. This issue was escalating by the minute. Special reports were coming in of power outages in other cities, the news was sketchy and no one could find any pattern or reason for this phenomenon. One announcer dramatically phrased his report, "Fear was mounting, fear of the unknown, the irrational, the unexplainable." The reporter signed off saying, "There is nothing to fear, but fear itself."

Lost in this frenzy of news reporting and news making was a small item involving the overflow of the Sakuma Dam on the Tenyu River.

The report read 12.20 a.m. "One person dead two missing when flood waters overran the Sakuma Dam. The man made lake was swollen due to recent abnormally snowfall up river. As the river rushed towards the narrows of the dam, an eight foot wall of water hit the dam and nearby buildings causing flooding. The automatic spill gates designed to allow excess water to run off failed to operate. One man was washed away as thousands of gallons of freezing cold water cascaded over the dam. No reason was given for the failure of the spill gates. Still in some danger are houses and wildlife further down river." The Newscaster flipped pages so the drama would not be rushed. "The dam, built about 30 years ago, is 500 feet high and was designed to hold two hundred and sixty nine million cubic feet of water. Its' computerized control systems were updated in the late 1980's to bring them up to world standards and had never experienced problems before. Currently there are no fears of the dam's collapse but engineers are monitoring the situation. Police are searching for bodies!" A brief pause. "The authorities in Japan are confused about a sudden spate of "accidents" and are unable to provide any explanation to quell the rising panic." The words sounded ominous.

Tom's brow furrowed deeply as he listened to the broadcasts and he became very disturbed.

CHAPTER 7

One hundred thousand tons of steel ploughed steadily through heavy seas at 16 knots enroute to Hawaii. The twenty-five foot waves and forty mile per hour winds pounded the ship relentlessly as it crashed through the angry South Pacific Ocean. Designed to withstand much worse weather the crew of the Tanami felt comfortable that their usual run from Melbourne to Hawaii would be nothing more than routine.

"Steady as she goes," First Officer Stanton instructed the helm as he peered out into the murky blackness of this December 31st. He steadied himself as the ship rolled again yielding to the immense force of the storm.

Built in 1970 at the famous Swan Hunters Shipyard, Wallsend, England. The Tanami, first launched as Hercules, had been the pride of the fleet of Brown Brothers Shipping Line. This bulk carrier was an engineer's marvel when built and was originally intended to ship fruit and beef products from South America to Europe in refrigerated storage. Considered the state of the art, when launched, it was one of the last large ships to be built on Tyneside. Fierce competition from Japan and Korea and an inflexible union labor had ensured the slow death of the once famous shipbuilders, who boasted, once, that they could build a one million-ton oil tanker.

After fifteen years service, the Hercules was laid up, as trade with Argentina and Britain slowed due to economic instability and eventually the Falkland Islands conflict. The Australian Shipping Company, ASC. purchased Hercules in 1982 from the liquidators of Brown Brothers.

Although past its best Hercules was a bargain. ASC paid a fraction of what it would have cost to build, even after a refit in Germany's Hamburg Ship Repair Yard. Once again this majestic ship became the pride of the fleet, albeit a small Australian fleet. The hull and superstructure of the ship was well designed and needed very little modification; however, the power units were updated with the latest computerized controls and monitoring systems. These systems were designed to optimize the energy efficiency of the old engines and nothing escaped the scrutiny of sophisticated electronic surveillance devices, which ensured that correct operating and maintenance conditions always prevailed. Any non-performing part would automatically be taken out of service before any major damage occurred and warning lights alerted the engineers. Consequently Hercules now renamed Tanami was the most efficient ship operating in the South Pacific Ocean.

The crew was proud of their ship and their long record of high productivity as the Tanami produced more profit per sea miles than another other Australian registered ship. This pride was supplemented by the fact that they enjoyed better pay than any other ship they knew.

Being at sea on New Years Eve was not a hardship to most of the crew, few had long-standing relationships. Only the captain and chief engineer were married and two of the crew was engaged to be married when the next bonuses were paid in February 2000. Of the twenty-five-member crew, four were on watch. First Officer Jim Stanton, and three ratings, this was routine in a fully automated ship but with the heavy seas each man remained a little more alert.

"Helm amidships" Stanton instructed, bracing himself against the brass compass, in anticipation of the ships fall.

"Aye, Aye, Sir!" the automatic answer was lost in the noise of the storm.

The captain and second officer had retired to their cabins and were trying to sleep as the Tanami crashed through the waves, relentlessly moving northeast its speed cut to fourteen knots. The remainder of the crew was in the mess, celebrating the beginning of the new millennium.

John Francis, the Chief Engineer was drunk, not falling down drunk, but reflectively drunk, as he consoled himself with a bottle of scotch for being absent from his family on this New Year's Eve, a special day for the Scottish. At fifty five he was one of the few crewmembers who was tired of the sea and looking forward to retirement in two years. Joining the merchant navy at seventeen his forty years at sea would qualify him for a comfortable pension at fifty-seven.

John was a craggy man of Scottish decent. His iron gray hair brushed straight back and bushy eyebrows gave his age away. His green eyes, now bloodshot, stared intensely at the bottle of whiskey; heavy lids gave the impression he was sleepy. He had a weakness for scotch when not on duty and now sat, ruddy faced carving a hole in a bottle of Glenfidich.

Francis had served under many captains and was considered a good engineer; always able to cope with the most complicated mechanical problems. His Achilles heel was in the computer side of the business, although fully trained with the equipment he was not in the least interested in the high tech aspects of the job, preferring to rely on the junior officers to keep a watchful eye on the gizmos. John Francis was of the old school and prided himself that when the electronics failed he would come to the rescue with simple tried and tested mechanical solutions.

The rest of the crew sat around the mess in various stages of drunkenness talking in small groups but the overall mood was quiet. Christmas carols provided the background noise making everyone reminisce about their recent shore leave, which had ended on schedule three days ago.

John reached for the bottle of Glenfidich as he glanced at the clock fixed to the mess wall.

"Less than a minute to go before another century disappears into history," he thought. He liberally poured the whiskey into his glass securely held by his large scarred hands. As midnight approached he stood and raised his glass to his colleagues and simply said "Happy Hogmanay to ye all, all the best to you and yours" he took a long slug of the whiskey and sat down.

The crew returned the sentiment. "Happy New Year" was repeated amongst the clinking of glasses.

The mood picked up as if new hope had entered the room along with the new millennium. Francis staggered to his feet again, determined to make another toast, he held on to the back of his chair and began to raise his glass. Suddenly the ship shuddered, and seemed to move in reverse as if some giant hand had pushed it back. The lights flickered then went out completely. Bodies were tossed about the mess like rag dolls. The ship rolled again crashing noises filled the mess and the men waited in the darkness expecting the lights to return. if not by the main generator, then by the emergency one. The storm had blackened out any hope of moonlight and in the total darkness, the sounds of the ship straining to resist the waves were amplified. Straining noises gave the impression that two forces were locked together in mortal combat for supremacy, the sea trying to claim another victim and the ship fighting for survival. The sound of breaking glass added to the chaos, bottles and tumblers hit the floor of the mess. The ship moved erratically as if some monstrous child was playing with it, pushing it wildly around the sea.

"Shit! I've been cut," a voice slurred in the darkness.

Panic entered the bridge along with the darkness. First Officer, James Stanton (Jim) was not prepared for this loss in power and cursed. He hesitated and struggled to dredge up any remnants of training, which would cover this situation. "What the hell is going on," he shrieked.

"Helm's not answering, Sir."

Stanton picked up the phone and screamed into the mouthpiece, he waited several seconds for a reply from the engine room before he realized there was no power. He fell to the floor; the one hundred thousand-ton ship may well have been a toy as far as the sea was concerned, for it bobbed like a cork at the mercy of the massive waves.

Captain Whitely was on the bridge immediately. "Status report Mr. Stanton?"

"Lost all power around midnight, Sir" was his brief reply, "no damage sustained yet":

"Get a message off, with our position, as soon as possible, just in case," instructed the Captain calmly. "Quickly man and get the engineers busy, there can't be much wrong," he shouted above the noise of the storm.

Grabbing the first flashlight he could, Stanton scrambled off the bridge, to find John Francis and get the radio operator in action. He glanced at Whitely, before he left the bridge and marveled at his calmness.

Captain Whitely was a tall lean figure who exuded confidence. He had been at sea all his life and had risen from cabin boy at sixteen to Captain in his forty-year career. This was not the worst situation he had been in, although the total loss of power was disconcerting, he was sure it was only temporary.

"What's our position," he asked the helmsman.

"Last time Mr. Stanton looked it was Latitude 171 and Longitude 24," the helmsman replied.

He was pouring over the navigation charts, using a hand held flashlight, which pierced the darkness and flooded several square feet with light. Since he had left the bridge some four hours before he knew roughly the ships position and that they were in the area of the Minerva Reefs, but that did not immediately concern him.

He was more concerned about the security of the cargo as these seas would be ruthless on anything shaken loose.

"Hold her into the wind."

"Helm does not respond Sir."

In contrast to the calmness on the bridge it was chaos in the mess. One of the ratings had located the emergency flashlight and the thin ray made the picture look like a scene from a horror movie. Only John Francis was moving, struggling to diagnose the situation through a whiskey fog. He was moving out of the mess trying to get to the engine room when Jim met him.

"What the hell happened?" slurred John, as he fought to keep his balance as the ship lurched from side to side.

"Lost all power at midnight, no reason, just nothing, no warning, no nothing."

John pushed past Jim and staggered into a dark corridor.

"Here take this" he heard from behind as the First Officer thrust the flashlight into his right hand.

Jim made his way into the mess shouting for Gibson the radio operator.

"Gibson, where the hell are you?"

"He's here sir," replied someone in the darkness. Jim looked at the body rolling about the mess on the floor; Gibson was out cold his head bleeding. Gibson was out of action.

"Morris get your ass into the radio room and prepare to broadcast our location. You will have to use the emergency battery until we get things back to normal" Morris was moving cautiously through the darkness.

"I'll get the position down to you as soon as possible," he heard from behind.

Morris needed a flashlight and found his way to the galley where he knew there were several, and easily located them in the darkness by the flashing red lights. He made his way slowly to the radio room and began to switch on the equipment. The dials jumped alive and spread a soft glow across the room as the emergency battery kicked in silently. By the time he was ready the First Officer was there with the ships estimated position.

"Get this off as soon as possible

    Longitude 171 degrees 15 degrees

    Latitude 24 degrees 37 degrees"

Jim said matter of fact and handed Morris a torn piece of paper with the potentially life saving scribble.

Morris set to work at the radio wondering who on earth would be monitoring radio messages on New Years Eve.

CHAPTER 8

Deep in a nondescript government office in Arlington, Virginia, U.S.A., Raymond Bennett browsed through the brief intelligence reports that had trickled in through the night. Business, as expected, was slow due to the impending arrival of a New Year, indeed the New Millennium, in about eighteen hours. He scanned the documents briefly and shook his head slowly, torn between them and his own personal thoughts. The upcoming change in the millennium had caused many to reflect on their past, Raymond Bennett was no different.

"Wonder where Jon is now" he could not shake his sense of guilt. "Would I recognize him if I met him?" he challenged himself. "What was he doing now?" many unanswered questions floated through his mind.

He let his memory wander back to that fateful day, over twenty years ago, when he left his brother at the orphanage without even having the chance to say goodbye. The image was painful and his subconscious tried to protect him from the pain. He looked at his watch through misty eyes 6.12 a.m. he noted.

"Um! Less than an hour to go!" His mood brightened as he anticipated finishing his shift and beyond that his date with Sally Damen in about twelve hours, to celebrate this special new year's eve. His chair scraped hard against the floor, as he pushed back from the desk, stood up and walked over the world map hanging on the wall of his office. He studied intently the red flags, used to depict official security areas, and tapped the outline of Iraq, the only location that had both a red flag and a brief report now lying on his desk. He recollected the message.

"Small troop activity noted around Rumalia not large enough to pose a threat!"

His eyes moved over the map again, dismissing Iraq from his thoughts he looked at the other potential trouble spots highlighted by other red flags.

Raymond let his mind ruminate;" The Bosnian crisis was no longer center stage, Dissidents in the ever-freer China were becoming more active but posed no threat to world peace as yet. India continued in its' quest to find political stability, together with a peaceful coexistence with Pakistan. The two countries had proved to each other their nuclear prowess and therefore were on equal terms in the race to destruction. The only real dark clouds were the volatility of the Anglo-Irish talks on a united Ireland, however, with the large scale disarming of the Irish Republican Army in early 1999 there was no immediate fear of a return to terrorism." However, the new splinter group the "Irish Liberation Army" or ILA was a new and unknown cause for concern.

With this background of relative world harmony he did not expect the reports in front of him to hold any excitement.

Raymond had pulled night duty for the last two months and was coming to the end of his working day on this Friday December 31. He was looking forward to a long weekend with Sally, starting with a party tonight. Raymond felt remarkably fresh as he had managed to nap in his dingy, windowless office, buried in the basement of the large nondescript office complex. His thoughts drifted between the uninteresting reports scattered over his small desk and his life in the CIA. The reality of the job did not meet his original expectations and Raymond often found himself in a reflective mood lately. The slowness of the nightshift gave him more time to think about his life, his future, and now a renewed friendship with Sally Damen. These thoughts danced around his mind as he unconsciously shuffled the piles of paper around his small, aged desk.

Raymond Bennett had spent his early years in California in the San Francisco area after being adopted by Robert and Mary Bennett when he was eight years old, a process he again painfully remembered that had separated him from his brother. Both Bennetts were compassionate about Raymond's start in life and invited him to call them father and mother, which Raymond did reluctantly.   Mrs. Bennett doted on Raymond, as if he were her own son, and gave him everything she could as if compensating some penance for past misdeeds. Mr. Bennett disagreed with her doting ways but acquiesced to her will, occasionally showing periodic frustration towards Raymond's influence over her. Sometimes he tried to compensate for his wife's overindulgence which resulted in a forced relationship with his adopted son, however, he was basically a kind man and loved Raymond in his own reserved way.

The Bennett's were considered comfortable, Robert worked as an Air Traffic Controller in San Francisco International Airport, and Mary was a substitute teacher in the Town of Milbrae in San Mateo. They lived in a three-bedroom, split-level, house on a well-manicured lot measuring one hundred feet deep by fifty feet wide. It was similar to all the other houses on Franklin Street differentiated mainly by its gray colored cedar shake siding. The ground level held a one car garage and Raymond's bedroom, the second level comprised of a lounge, dining room and kitchen and above the ground level rooms were two bedrooms, a den and a bathroom. The house was large enough to give Raymond some privacy, which he never took for granted after the cramped facilities of the orphanage.

Raymond's school life was almost idyllic, he integrated well, partially due to his bright lively nature but mainly because everyone knew his new mother and went out of their way to help him. His new found stability helped Raymond add the quality of confidence to his personality however, Mary always sensed there was something missing. She acted as a bridge between Raymond and Robert hoping that the two men would form their own relationship, but it proved difficult for both of them! Family outings to nearby Candlestick Park and trips to Disneyland were always successful, but never really broke down the invisible barriers between the males. She even bought Raymond a short wave radio set so he could listen to the pilots and air traffic controllers' banter as they guided the thousands of people into and out of San Francisco air space. This common interest did improve their relationship much to the delight of Mary.

By his graduation from high School his stunning good looks, blonde hair and ready smile had won the hearts of many young women. They envied his deep blue eyes and long eyelashes, they reveled in his sense of humor and his attentiveness to their needs. Their ultimate seduction usually occurred in his bedroom after listening to the emergency police calls on his premier ADI VHF radio. A few drinks and the brief peak into the town and county's underworld activity inevitably broke down any girl's resistance, and he became known as "The Radio Ram." This nickname brought an unashamedly wry smile to his face every time he heard it.

Choosing a college in California did not appeal to Raymond, and he looked eastward for his undergraduate life, partly to escape what was becoming a stifling life and partly, to find his brother, who he assumed would be still in the Newark area. He applied to Harvard and MIT as his primary targets, and Boston University and Boston College were his back ups.

His first real disappointment in life came in the summer of 1991 when he failed to get into either of his first choice colleges.

There was no real explanation as to why his one in eleven chance had not materialized, but there he was in the company of ten other equivalent students who did not make it either, so he did not brood over this.

Boston College, based in Newton, Massachusetts, became the new focus of his life for four years, at least academically; socially Raymond matured around the bars and restaurants of Boston. His first year had been a struggle as he, like all freshmen, adjusted to his life on Newton campus situated about a mile and a half from Boston College's main campus. He spent the first three weeks tripled up in a two-person dorm room situated in a block called Duchesne and found it difficult to adjust to the overcrowding. To supplement his parents financial support, Raymond found work on "Upper Campus," serving drinks in Alumni House, which was close to his dorm. The work was fun and the camaraderie between current and past students was a unique experience for him. The Alumni members encouraged the student barmen to imbibe with them, resulting in many humorous hours of work. Although Duchesne and Alumni House were only 100 yards apart, there were times when Raymond could not make it to the dorm and was found sleeping it off propped under a tree between the two buildings.

His reputation grew, but in the wrong areas and with all these distractions, his first year results failed to meet with his or the school's expectations. His parents also were disappointed, but Mrs. Bennett's indulgence, as always, prevailed when it came to Raymond, and he made it, just barely to the sophomore year.

With a stern warning from the Dean of the Business School, seconded by his father, Raymond returned to Boston College in late August and spent the next two years off campus in private apartments located on Cleveland Circle close to the main campus. He roomed with four other students and settled down to work for his degree in business and computer science. His inquisitive mind led him to the forefront of the technological revolution and he became skilled in the latest system trends.

Technology became a narcotic to him, and he absorbed it like a sponge.

His senior year was half way over before he knew it, and suddenly he felt he was on a collision course with reality, the end of his carefree days were clearly in sight. He indulged in the usual rounds of on-campus interviews, arranged with Fortune 500 company representatives and as computer science graduates were hot property, Raymond was hot property. He accepted offers to visit several companies including a relatively small industrial conglomerate called Underplan and Hope, Inc. based in New Jersey and Global Insurance Corp.; a huge financial company based in Boston. The contrast could not have been greater between the advanced technology used by Global and the dated philosophy and systems used at "Underplan". Based on this sample of two visits, Raymond elected to join the insurance business, after graduating magna cum laude.

His initial position within Global Insurance Corp. was in the Information Management Department as a trainee systems analyst. In this position he interfaced with hard-bitten computer experts, long ago disillusioned by the unreasonable demands of the business world. The contrast between Raymond's enthusiasm and his older colleague's cynicism resulted in many good-humored discussions.

"You're just a bunch of cynics!" Raymond teased a small discontented audience of programmers sitting around the lunch table.

"You'll learn soon enough son!" A weary voice replied "And remember cynic is another word for realistic!" he added.

"Life 's getting too fast for you guys!" Raymond went on "Your customers know more than you do!'

"They think they do! We have to pull it all together and make it work. There is no bridging the gap between system user expectations and what we can provide, especially within the timescale, budget and resources allotted." Another joined in. "The common theory, bought into by many, was that the MIS Department only deals in failure, remember MIS does not stand for Management Information Systems but "Missing Information Systems." He added with a smirk on his face.

They all laughed.

"If a systems project is a success it's because of the users, if it is a failure its because of the MIS Department", he stared knowingly at Raymond while the others nodded and smiled. Therefore, by deduction, we deal in failure!"

"You've heard of the title CIO, haven't you Raymond?" another asked.

"Yes". Raymond answered tentatively.

"I bet you think it stands for Chief Information Officer?" he looked at Raymond unsmiling, "But we know it stands for Career Is Over." They all laughed at this "in joke" as they rose from lunch to do battle one more time.

Insurance companies relied heavily on retaining claims information for statistical as well as historical reasons and their computer systems were the backbone of this archiving ability. Raymond learned that these large and complex systems had been designed and built in the nineteen sixties and seventies and used a now obsolete programming language called 'Cobol' or 'Common Business Language.' The original life span of these systems was expected to be a lot less than thirty years. However, the majority of companies modified the old systems to cope with their changing business needs, consequently much of the old technology was still around in nineteen ninety five, long past it's sell-by date, so to speak.

The larger U.S. companies became concerned about this due to a small inherent, but crucial, problem on how the systems calculate and store dates. This glitch would make all dates after the year 2000 read as 1900 and cause miscalculations and computer breakdowns. Governments and companies began a long and slow remediation plan to correct this problem. This effort became known as the 'Y2K' or 'Millennium Bug' project.

In nineteen ninety five, the major MIS efforts at Global were to merge the systems of its newly acquired subsidiary Triton Insurance and to modify all existing programming code, which had date sensitive information, to become Y2K compliant. Both efforts were a monumental task, requiring massive focus and resources, however, the merger deadline was closer, therefore the integration of the two systems took priority, leaving the Y2K project in a secondary role.

Raymond's tasks were divided between the two projects and, for the first six months, he experienced the frustration of being a small cog in a large, rapidly moving wheel. Although he learned a great deal, he felt no sense of identity or accomplishment with these major projects as they lumbered onward seemingly with a life of their own. Overarching this activity was the continual day to day requirements of the business, which demanded even more systems effort. "It was like changing the tires on a moving car, even worse, an accelerating car," he thought and began to understand the cynic's point of view. He was beginning to feel disillusioned with his career choice, and regretted joining Global Insurance.

The commercialization of the Internet reinvigorated him, stimulated by the phrase "Information Superhighway" coined by Vice President Al Gore, this prompted the development and a whole new generation of technology and Raymond developed these skills immediately. He also began looking for a position in another department.

During his early months with Global, he had attended several orientation sessions to learn about the responsibilities and functions of the many other departments within the organization and had mentally targeted a few of them as desirable career destinations. One such target was Market Research, which not only used modern technology but also seemed to have a monopoly on the cute young women of the company. One, in particular, Sally Damen, looked very appealing to him. She was blonde, blue eyed, 5-ft. 4", bundle of fun who seemed to be popular with everyone. His initial advances were met with indifference, which was a new experience for him, no woman had resisted his attentions with such lightness, and his confidence began to fade when in her presence. His ego was bruised continuously so much so he began to avoid her at all costs preferring to concentrate on past girlfriends for dates.

Apprehension and elation vied for his attention when his superior, Ed Ward informed him that he had been assigned to the market research department to help them develop an Internet Capability. Ward began, "In large companies, it is usual to assemble a multi-disciplined team to develop individual business solutions. This project will bring a team of seven people together." Ward mentioned some familiar and some unfamiliar names, but most of the briefing was a blur after Sally Damen's name had been mentioned.

Raymond's first thoughts were to try and duck out of the project but he balanced this irrational fear of Sally with the disillusionment of his current assignment and tentatively agreed to participate. The next days were a mixture of anticipation and apprehension as Raymond waited for the first team meeting to be called. Notification that the meeting would be held at 9 a.m. June 23 in the blue conference room on the 3rd floor came in the form of an e-mail. He read the note and stared at the monitor, a blank look on his face meant that his mind had drifted to some unknown destination. "Wish I'd side stepped this one," he thought.

The phone rang, jolting him from his subconscious isolation and he lunged at the receiver. "Bennett here!" he shouted into the receiver.

Sally, startled by his loudness asked jokingly "Did I wake you up?'

Raymond found himself holding his breath unable to speak. "Er ... no, no." he stammered.

Sally continued "Can we meet for lunch today to discuss ideas about the project."

Fighting for composure he managed a weak "O.K.", jotting down the time of their meeting, then circling it continuously. Raymond slowly replaced the receiver and felt completely stunned, he allowed himself to exhale slowly almost whistling through his teeth. The morning dragged until it was time to make his way to the cafeteria on the 8th floor. Mexican food was today's theme; Sombreros hung everywhere as Raymond scanned the arriving faces for Sally. It was a three-minute wait before the effervescent face appeared and smilingly greeted him, then immediately moved towards the food,

"I'm starving," she said.

He was swept along with her enthusiasm choosing the same as she did, chicken soup, garden salad and coke, and followed her across the cafeteria, noting with approval the way her short cotton skirt tightened over her hips as she walked.

They found a seat in a corner, Raymond placed his food tray down on the table while Sally waved and acknowledged several people nearby, it was clear she enjoyed extensive popularity. This gave Raymond time to compose himself as he looked dolefully at her. Her round face was framed with short golden hair. Her blue eyes were alive absorbing everything around her. Her nose was perfect, slightly upturned and her lips were full, framing a small mouth, which constantly smiled. She had a perfectly sculpted figure and he could not take his eyes from her breasts, which peaked through a taut white shirt.

"How are you today?" Sally finally turned towards him.

"Fine and you?"

"Great! Just great!" she oozed.

His mouth felt dry and he sipped his coke.

"Are you excited about the project" she quizzed, her eyes narrowed.

"Don't know that much about it really" he related matter-of-factly.

Sally leaned forward spooning her soup idly Raymond thought that the buttons on her blouse would surely snap and watched intently.

"We want to set up Internet sites to perform market research and customer satisfaction questionnaires!" she explained.

"That seems simple enough!" Raymond said dryly, trying hard not to stare at her breasts again.

"We want to do this quickly!" Sally paused to taste the chicken soup.

Raymond responded, "seems easy enough!" he felt stupid repeating himself.

"Difficulty is that ... the project overlaps both the marketing department and customer service department!" Sally broke in nervously, she did not look at him.

"I'm not sure why this would be a difficulty." Raymond thought out aloud.

"Well!" Sally drawled screwing up her pretty face, in a word "politics" she whispered, "or should I say rivalry!" She bent towards Raymond emphasizing the last word.

"What can I do?" he asked in a bewildered voice.

"Er... we would like it kept a secret until we have something real to show people!" Sally explained, hesitantly, concentrating on stirring her soup.

Raymond's senses were alert now as he began to realize the reason for Sally's call. He was disappointed but did not show it. "Nothing life threatening here either way," he thought". "But if we bring the other departments in we'll have more resources" he added logically showing his politically naive side.

Sally looked uncomfortable now still avoiding direct eye contact. "It's not played that way!" she ventured and he watched as her bubbly personality turned flat. She was obviously laboring in this conversation now and he wanted to release the tension.

"Seems ok by me" he said, quickly watching the relief spread over her face. She smiled weakly.

"I'm not very good at this" she said honestly, "I was elected to talk to you but I cannot see the point either, if you don't want to go along with it I wouldn't blame you," she paused. The truth is the two directors are eligible for promotion and this might give my boss the edge, it's as simple as that."

Raymond had a sense of relief at Sally's admission and understood the politics. He leaned over the table and placed his hand over hers,

"It's no big deal."

Sally's zest for life returned and they both enjoyed the remainder of the lunch agreeing to meet for dinner next week.

Raymond thought his luck had changed. He genuinely liked Sally and wanted to know more about her. The rest of the day passed by in a haze of confused thoughts and he hoped this was the beginning of a beautiful relationship.

The project lasted three months and ended in success, the team gained company wide accolades, for adopting the latest technology to improve customer service. The end of the project meant a loss of direction for Raymond; he yearned for something more exciting and could not see the Global Insurance Corp. satisfying his longer term needs. Only Sally gave him a purpose in life now and he lived for the time they were together.

While out with her at Sissy Kays near Fanuel Hall celebrating her recent promotion, he bumped into an old college friend Bob Fulman who joined them for drinks. Memories were resurrected and elaborated over the constant flow of tequila sunrises, as the two reminisced about their undergraduate life at, BC, Sally noticed that Raymond was full of life again, his eyes gleaming with excitement as he relived his past escapades. The contrast of this new found zest with the dullness of today's experiences burdened them both momentarily. They looked into each other's eyes and realized instantly that something was missing. His imagination really caught fire when Bob revealed that he worked for the CIA and began to talk about some of the cases he had worked on. Raymond hung on his every word and Sally recognized that Raymond's days with Global were numbered.

It was five months later that Raymond, full of hope and anticipation, walked through the doors of the CIA and was directed to his small office to gather information.

CHAPTER 9

At 2.55 a.m. Jon decided to clear his head by walking along the beach. He tried switching on the apartments' lights without success.

"Must be the damned fuse," he muttered under his breath.

He squinted around the darkened room for his shoes, accidentally came across his wallet, which he tucked into the rear pocket of his old Levi jeans. He sat down and donned the worn pair of Nike sneakers, leaving the laces untied. Stretching as he stood up, he tried to shake the tired and edgy feeling that had overcome him. The apartment walls seem to close in on him as he made his way to the front door and quietly opened it.

The air was clear, he stepped outside and was relieved to escape the stale atmosphere of the building. Sounds of the celebration were all around him as he stumbled down to the beach and walked aimlessly around, "Some New Years Eve," he thought. "The biggest event this millennium and here I am out of it completely."

He had a sudden urge for a cigarette, a habit he had given up years ago, and he headed for the nearest vending machine. On his way he checked his wallet and decided to draw some money from the ATM machine in Westpark Bank, about a hundred meters away.

The night was warm and the slight sea breeze brought a calming effect to Jon as he padded over the sand to the promenade, then over the road to the darkened storefronts. Although it was light enough for him to determine where he was and where he was going, something made him feel uneasy but he could not put his finger on it.

He reached the ATM and inserted his card. The machine demanded his PIN and the amount of withdrawal, which he punched in automatically. The screen froze with the last command, as he waited for it to scan for the necessary approvals through the complex system hidden behind the scene. Unable to find any valid instructions the ATM spat Jon's card out unceremoniously and closed down without any explanation, leaving him staring at his own reflection in the empty screen. Jon was bemused as he withdrew the card and scanned it for an obvious reason for this rejection, "looks o.k. to me!" he squinted hard, but it was too dark to read the usual details on the card. He lifted his head and looked around for better light and it was then that he realized that the only real light came from the moon. There was very little city lighting at all. The ever present winking of the red, amber and green traffic lights were clearly absent as he noticed sporadic drivers cautiously navigating the crossroads.

He turned in the direction of his apartment and sauntered back, lost in thought and with the distant beginnings of a hangover forming deep in his conscious mind. The edgy feeling still accompanied him and his intuition made him feel increasingly uneasy as he entered his apartment and noticed the remnants of the party that now seemed so long ago. He could see bodies lying all over the furniture and floor and he gingerly stepped over several as he made his way to the kitchen for a much-needed coffee. With the absence of electric power, he was grateful for the old gas stove; he searched for his lighter and a cigarette. He lit the stove first then a cigarette and sat down to wait for the coffee in the dimness of the moon light which cast a blue tinge through the windows. Jon sat quietly; staring at the gas flame hoping it would magically provide him with some answers. A shrill whistling noise filled the room; startled he jumped up, lifted the kettle off the heat and made a single mug of instant coffee. He sat down again and sipped the strong brew. The coffee burnt his lips causing him to curse. He sat back in the chair a sense of foreboding flooded over him, he shivered then stood up and crept gingerly to his bedroom.

He felt that in a better mental condition he could begin to understand the recent events, but the explanations were just outside his sphere of reasoning for the time being. The darkened room infuriated him; the only power available was the small standby battery, which powered his radio during power outages. Kneeling on the floor, he leaned over and switched on the radio, the soft light from the dials threw out a comforting golden glow over the immediate area. He sat down in front of the set and unconsciously took out his credit card again to inspect it. It looked in order. Expiration date August 8, 2001 appeared to be valid and he vaguely conjured up Stanley Kubricks movie "2001 A Space Odyssey". The haunting music filled his mind. Impulsively he decided to call customer service at the number on the back of the credit card to check, however, after several failed attempts he gave up, in frustration.

His headache was getting worse so he searched for some Panadol tablets and finished his coffee with two tablets. It was 3.15 a.m. now so he decided to check in with Tom and automatically dialed "Roadrunners" frequency.

"Tom here" he answered immediately dispensing with the normal handles.

"Can't sleep either!" Jon challenged,

"Nope," came the somber reply.

"Something's up and I can't get my mind around it," whispered Jon.

"Yeah there are some strange goings on all right," Tom thought aloud.

"What do you mean?" quizzed Jon?

"Well, besides the mysterious aircraft and the distress calls from an unknown ship somewhere in the nearby Pacific, Japan has problems with their railways and a dam has mysteriously overflowed."

Jon sat slowly taking this in whilst playing with his credit card. "I am sure there is a reasonable explanation but I can't think of one!" Jon muttered.

"Besides these mysteries, Tom added, I came across a message confirming a ninety nine million dollar transfer to Sydney at 11.55 p.m." "Strange timing!" - the words hung in the airwaves.

Jon focused on his credit card more intently, 2001 loomed large, 2001 - HAL the computer had taken over the space ship in the movie. In the background he heard Tom rambling on about the Caledonia power outages.

"Jesus Christ" Jon screamed, "Jesus Christ! …That's it!"

Tom shuddered at the revelation but was clueless "What? What?" he demanded.

"It's Millie!" Jon shrieked his voice so high pitched it was almost as if it were helium induced.

"Who?" Tom screamed, "Who?"

"Millie! Millie!" Jon repeated, the words gushing out over his dry tongue.

"It's the millennium bug."

"You all right?" questioned Tom.

"Yeah, for the first time tonight" Jon squawked, fighting to get his normal voice back.

"Calm down, calm down!" Tom demanded.

"What the hell are you talking about, has the booze addled your brain?"

"It has been until now" Jon interrupted, "but it just got clearer!"

"Listen, back in the 1960s computer programming was difficult and expensive, or to be more exact, the storage of data was expensive, so programmers used short cuts to optimize a computer's memory. One of those short cuts was to use two digits for the year in the date, for example December 25, 1964 became 122564."

"You know that?" Jon challenged.

"Yeah!" Tom replied unenthusiastically not willing to show his ignorance.

"Well in the 1970's the insurance companies were using computer systems to forecast out 30 years for life assurance purposes," Jon continued. "The results of these calculations were rubbish because the system read 00 year as 1900 and not 2000!" Jon instructed.

Tom knew that Jon knew what he was talking about, but he was lost.

"Take it from the beginning," Tom interrupted. "I'm a little slow this morning!"

Jon slowed down and began to explain the problem more logically.

"Computers work by a series of written instructions which we term programs. These programs tell the computer what to do and how to do it." Jon slowed again searching for the right words. "Consider that you are aged 54 in the year 2,000. A computer would take your birth date in 1946 and subtract it from 2000 and calculate you to be 54 years old, right?"

"Right," reiterated Tom.

"OK, due to a glitch in programming way back, a computer will read the year 2000 as 1900. So when the same calculation is done now it will take 1946 away from 1900 leaving minus 46. It may convert the minus sign to a plus giving 46, but in both cases the answer is wrong." Jon paused. " In modern integrated systems this incorrect data will be automatically transferred to other calculations and hence the errors will be compounded. At best there will be grossly incorrect calculations and at worst the system will crash or no longer be operative."

Tom's continued silence was evidence enough that Jon had made his point.

"Now the world has known about this problem for over thirty years but everyone expected that these 1970 programs would be replaced by now. It was a huge problem; some early tests revealed that on average over seventy percent of these programs would be affected. Companies, pressured by priorities were reluctant to address the problem until the late 1990s when resources were in so much demand that it became impossible to complete the projects in time. In fact, resources were so tight that there was a great fear that rogue programmers would take shortcuts and hide the problem without solving it!"

He paused, waiting for Tom to ask a question, silence dominated the airwaves, so he continued. "Even in 1997 experts predicted that over twenty percent of the worlds' systems would not be year 2,000 compliant. These same experts compared the effort of manpower and money with World War II, it is that big!"

Jon was clear headed now; either the panadol or rush of adrenaline was working.

Tom was enthralled; he butted in "I can understand how

insurance companies are affected but what about our mysteries?"

Jon continued. "In the 1980s and 1990s, computer chips were used to control everything, for instance elevators. When an elevator is maintained the next scheduled date is recorded in its system. It also monitors itself for mechanical problems. If the system identifies a weakness or a missed maintenance date it automatically records this and puts itself out of service. Some early tests on elevators were accomplished by inserting a date over the year 2,000 caused them to travel to the basement and close down. This same logic can control aircraft, ships, trains etc., etc., Even the most basic of needs in power will be controlled in some shape or form by microchips and one dysfunctional transfer of data will compromise the systems. Prison doors or bank vault doors could be flung open or closed indefinitely, blood banks controlled by computers will be in chaos as dates become invalid, and they order good product destroyed!"

Jon stared at his radio for a moment then continued. "The problem was not only identifying the programming code, which needs to be fixed, but also any and all changes need to be tested by the users of the systems to ascertain that the output is correct. This testing effort was about sixty percent of the whole project, and the people usually have to do this in addition to performing their ordinary duties, whole organizations were under tremendous stress, so you can see how errors could occur."

"Tom whistled through his teeth, "How did we get in this mess?" he groaned.

Jon added more; "The enormity of the problem was never fully understood until too late, systems were so integrated that no one realized where the interfaces of data really were. The world had become so dependent on data from different sources, which grew over decades, that we never fully considered all the consequences!" He took another pause for breath.

"Governments left the problem for big business to solve. The only leadership they provided was issuing SEC rules making companies record their costs and liabilities relating to the Y2K, and who was going to admit that they were not compliant with all the legal and insurance ramifications!"

Tom shook his head in disbelief. " I really can't get my head around this!"

Jon continued "It was ironic, because no government department was requested to make such a declaration, although it was known that the I.R.S. and F.A.A. were in trouble in 1997. The sin of the situation is that the problem was so well known that Government's and businesses alike needlessly wasted billions of dollars in remediation of the old systems. With a little more planning, new, more functional systems could have been implemented for little more!"

The summary Jon had just orated made him feel depressed and he sat drained and angry as he thought about the tremendous waste.

"Why did you name it Millie?" Tom queried.

"I didn't! some wiseass, in nineteen eighty-eight, did and it stuck, sort of fit, describing it like some innocuous bug which everyone underestimated. We should have called it 'Superbug' or something to catch everyone's attention."

"Well Professor" Tom broke in, " Now what do we do about it?"

"That my friend is another question altogether," Jon said subduely

"Some people have described this situation as rearranging deck chairs on the Titanic!"

"Too little, too late?" Tom queried.

"Something like that," Jon said reflectively.

CHAPTER 10

Raymond's thoughts drifted from reminiscing to the pile of reports lying on his desk from the far-flung regions of the world, he looked at his watch, 6.30 a.m. and yawned involuntarily.

He was looking forward to his date with Sally Damen this New Year's eve and this brought a playful smile to his face. Sally was normally based in Global Insurance's Boston Office but due to some heavy workloads experienced in their Washington Office for the year end, she had transferred down on temporary assignment. Both Raymond and Sally were happy to renew their long-standing friendship, if not romance, at such an exciting time.

Raymond's thoughts were interrupted by the latest batch of reports, which found their way to his desk via another weary analyst.

"Anything important?" he quizzed.

"Some small stuff," the analyst said disinterestedly and turned for the door, "I'm off home!" he added.

Raymond scanned the sketchy reports dredging up his early training to recognize any pattern or links to what appeared to be isolated instances and investigate these further.

1. The Kingfisher, a known gun running ship, has a registered destination as Honolulu. E.T.A., Hawaiian waters unknown.
2. Transport disruptions experienced in Japan. Dam overflow in Sakuma. Terrorist alert.
3. Large scale power outage in Sydney, Australia.

Seen in isolation these incidents did not appear to be significant; however, two previous messages had listed the possibility of a downed aircraft in Auckland, and sporadic power outages in New Zealand. The first report substantiated an old report that a large weapons transaction was pending, originally thought to involve the Irish Republican Army, or the newly formed. "Irish Liberation Army, the I.L.A."

Raymond's senses became sharpened immediately. Coincidences like these were too rare although he could see no feasible connection.

He decided to call a long-standing contact in the South Pacific area to confirm some of the statements. The telephone connection just would not go through although Raymond tried half a dozen times to connect to Noumea in the Coral Sea. He contacted the communications section to help him; they could not assist him in any conventional way but suggested the high frequency radio network. Raymond jumped at the idea and soon engaged Tom Ricer in a conversation about coincidences.

The CIA had recruited Tom in the late 1970's when Tom was known to associate with petty criminals and even pirates in the South China seas. These criminals never suspected him of being anything other than a half crazed and bitter refugee from the southern states of the U.S.A. Since his escape from Jakarta Tom had become equally comfortable growing poppies on some isolated God forsaken Island or at sea smuggling arms or drugs to anyone who would pay. He was known as a loner and not one you would purposely cross, but he kept to himself and was accepted by every low life in Southeast Asia.

Tom regularly passed information to the Agency on crucial movements of people and property and they passed the information to local government officials who made the occasional "bust" when their reputations needed a boost. The CIA also tipped Tom off when life was going to be uncomfortable for him and his friends, which kept Tom valuable to both sides of the law. With both sides paying Tom accumulated enough money to put a substantial down payment on his farm, but the main incentive was that the Agency suppressed information regarding his Navy record and so an uneasy alliance developed over the years.

Tom confirmed to Raymond the events that he was aware of in the region, adding also details about the distress call from the unknown ship. Almost by default he mentioned the strange transfer of ninety nine million dollars at five minutes before midnight. He also offered Jon's explanation about, "Millie the millennium bug." This immediately struck a cord with Raymond.

"Of course" he whispered during Tom's recital. "It all makes sense, even the fact that the telephone lines are experiencing difficulties" he continued. "The world is going to wake up with one hell of a hangover tomorrow" he mused, considering the real implications as they dawned on him.

His stomach had knotted up without him realizing it, and he was overcome with a sense of foreboding as the predictions of the issues flooded his memory. "The problem had been extensively publicized with widespread forecasts of failure. Indeed, the consequences of the unpredictable chain reaction, spawned by the system failures, would humble our technologically dependent society. Because of this, no government department, private or public business would dare admit anything other than complete compliance to their systems millennium change for fear of lawsuits." He paused for breath.

"Not again" Tom thought, he was weary and a little afraid of the outcome of this mumbo jumbo.

Raymond continued. "The suppression of the issue and the inevitable disparate opinions of the experts resulted in the general public throughout the world either unaware, or confused about the consequences that they would face as soon as they awakened on January 1, 2000.

"Speak English!" Tom interrupted him sharply.

Raymond smiled to himself, he found it difficult to 'Decomplex' the complex! He inhaled slowly. "The forecasts in the late nineties were that many people would face problems, ranging from the trivial, of not being able to make a telephone call or take money out of their bank accounts, to being in mortal danger of failed control equipment in homes, transport or factories." Silence again pervaded the air-waves. "Indeed nothing seemed to be safe on this collision course with destiny." Raymond added dramatically.

Tom Ricer had been educated almost beyond his capacity in the last hour or so. He was unaware that he had stopped breathing during Raymond's recitation. He gasped for air, still trying to understand the magnitude of the situation. To him the world seemed to be in imminent mortal danger, " Why is everyone so calm?" His mind churned as he asked.

Raymond could also not believe his own words. "It could not be true that mankind could find itself in this situation," he thought.

"The problem was not that all systems would fail, no, the real problem was that only some systems would fail, and the uncertainty that this random failure would have. The unknown and unpredictable was what to be feared." Raymond was in an expansive mood now,

Tom felt at a loss. He asked simply " What can be done?" The same question that had stumped Jon.

"It's beyond me…looks like we're too late!" Raymond said flatly

"Why was it so difficult?". Tom was fascinated.

"I'll try and explain it!" Raymond knew this was going to be difficult. " As computers became easier to use everyone assumed they had become less complicated, however the reverse is true. Try and picture a 'machine' with five 'layers' of complex operations, each interdependant on the other.

The first layer is what everyone sees, normally a P.C. with Microsoft's 'Windows.' This is used to present information in user friendly ways i.e. graphs, charts, etc. Let's call this the Presentation Level. Next is the Applications Level which collects data from many sources of input, manipulates it then sends it to storage. This storage is the next level; we call it a Database! These three levels are very complicated individually, however they are designed to constantly inter-react with each other, more complication!"

Raymond struggled for the right words.

"Any questions so far?"

"No!" Tom concentrated on the picture Raymond was painting.

"Now comes the hard part! The next layer is the Operating System, this tells the computer hardware what to do and when to do it! Don't ask any questions, as I do not understand this level at all! Finally there is the Network Level which allows all this to communicate, again this is a highly specialized field, so no questions! These five levels, collectively, is what most people call THE COMPUTER."

"OK so far?"

"Yeah!"

"As I said before, each level is complicated in itself, and each level has to inter-react with each other and here is the rub! Each level has elements that are date sensitive!"

Tom whistled though his teeth "Sounds like we were beaten before we started!"

"No! but we did not start soon enough!"

Raymond remembered his time with Global Insurance. "We even investigated the possibility of insuring against the Year 2000 Problem, several other companies were interested, but the cost of insurance was exorbitant. Not only that, the audit procedure to ensure companies complied with the best practices of solving the Y2K problem proved too onerous! Some companies were in denial of their system status and shied away from any chance to highlight their problems to the external world." Raymond paused. "The companies, which obtained insurance coverage for Y2K, were the companies who were more likely to successfully solve the problem," he added.

Tom interrupted, "Can you believe this shit?"

"It's difficult to comprehend, just too big!" Raymond paused for a moment.

"It gets worse, some of the early remedies chosen were to dupe the computer that the '00 date was 1900, this bought the company exactly 59 days because 2000 is a leap year and 1900 was not. February 29 would mean trouble to systems, like it did in 1996 when programmers missed the extra day, causing huge problems, lasting until January 1997."

Raymond fell silent; reflecting upon the difficulty it would be to convince anyone of influence that we were facing a real problem here, especially in the time available.

"It would be a case of kill the messenger and get on with the party."

His thoughts ran wild through his consciousness, creating havoc and fear. The issues flooded back into his mind, missed deadlines were common, legal issues regarding copyright law and software licenses were never resolved, consultants responsibilities etc., etc., The issues expanded exponentially.

Tom felt he had to contribute something to this grave situation, "Perhaps the ninety nine million dollar transfer was to save it in all this system confusion!"

Raymond's consciousness caught the drift of Tom's words, but the transfer of money was the one inconsistent event in the whole discussion. Raymond fought for the logic of that transfer, surely it would be safer to leave the money in a static record, which in theory should be easier to reconstruct in the event of any system failure. This transfer did not make sense to him at all now.

"Tom what were the details of that transaction, do you know?" quizzed Raymond.

"No, but I've got forty-five seconds of conversation on tape" he replied.

"Let's hear it!" posed Raymond.

As Tom was juggling with his controls to reproduce the tape, Raymond asked idly about Jon. Tom briefly repeated their conversation and how Jon, had explained the millennium problem to him.

"Sounds like a bright guy?" Raymond's statement came across like a question.

"Yeah!" Tom said, "he's bright!"

"Perhaps I should talk to him," Raymond responded, almost talking to himself.

"Yep, he's probably worth contacting," Tom responded.

"Here's the tape" he added and turned it on.

"Hi Colin, this is Pat. The scheduled transfer of ninety nine million dollars has been received by Sydney sorting code and account 710005 08 8006 04014268. The transfer to Hong Kong should occur at 3.55 a.m. Act. #810006 017007 05016289!"

Raymond closed his eyes as if to concentrate his senses on hearing. The instructions were very precise he thought. Why park money for four hours, why? Why? WHY?

On hearing it again Tom thought it even stranger.

Raymond asked. " Play it again? Better still wait and I'll record it," he added. The brief message was now in Virginia and Raymond signed off with a sense of purpose he had not experienced in a long time. "Oh! By the way, how can I contact Jon?"

Tom gave Raymond the details and signed off to have a stiff drink.

Raymond listened to the message over and over again. The only two crucial bits of data were the bank account numbers and possibly names, but how could he get more details. Time was ticking away. It was 9.35 a.m. and the office was well populated now. Everyone was in high spirits in anticipation of tonight's parties. They were mercifully unaware of Raymond's dilemma. Raymond walked over to Bill Drummond's desk where a balding, rotund figure sat putting his work in order.

Bill had a square face, strong jaw and his eyes were heavy lidded. Deep lines scarred his flesh and the skin on his neck sagged over his shirt collar. He had been part of the organization for thirty-four years and had once been in the field. It was hard to imagine Bill actively fighting the enemy's of the U.S.A., but looks are deceiving. Bill knew how the department operated and had contacts all over the world. He must have earned that respect somehow, but his story was never told, the unsung hero, no less.

"Hi Bill," Raymond greeted him.

"Hi Ray," Bill responded.

"What can I do for you?" As they had never really met socially Bill's intuition was right that this was not a social call.

"In last nights reports I came across two bank account numbers located in the Far East and wondered how I could check up on them?"

Raymond always found it best to be direct. It cut to the point and avoided any pretense of grace. Bill looked at his workload and looked at Raymond.

"Important eh?" he asked inquisitively, his eyes gleamed at the chance of excitement.

"Could be" Raymond replied, "but I'm not really sure, if they check out, I can go home and rest," he added.

Bill liked Raymond's directness and said to leave it with him. He did not promise anything but would do his best. Within forty-five minutes Bill caught up with Raymond at the coffeepot.

"Here's the information you wanted, don't ask any questions!" he thrust the folded paper into Raymond's hand and walked back to his desk.

Raymond stared at the paper.

>Account number 71000S 088006 0401268
>Global Bank Ltd.,
>Sydney, Australia

>Account number 810006 017007 05016289
>Global Bank Ltd.,
>Hong Kong

Global Bank is a wholly owned subsidiary of Global Insurance Company, a USA corporation.

Raymond walked slowly to his office, sat down, and picked up the phone and automatically dialed a number.

Sally had been at work for an hour and a half by the time Raymond called her. Jenny, Sally's secretary recognized Ray's voice immediately and put him through. Sally's eyes brightened as Ray began to speak. She really cared for him, but was not sure how he felt about her.

"How about me coming over for coffee?" he asked her immediately.

Taken by surprise she began to stutter excuses, but quickly conceded, smiling to herself "I'll clear you with security." She volunteered

Raymond ran out of his office and across the road to the parking lot, which held his current passion, a 1989 silver Cadillac Allante. This powerful two-seater was a true classic roadster, which turned every enthusiast's head. Raymond loved to drive this car to the limit; its responsive 4.5-liter engine coupled with its light aluminum body, gave it terrific performance. This particular model had a hard top for the cold months, and Raymond dutifully winterized the car every November. Come May the hard top was stored and it became a true convertible.

He moved out of the parking lot with a great deal of restraint, but once on the road, he effortlessly weaved in and out of the slower traffic to cut the driving time between his and Sally's office, down to twenty minutes. Security clearance in hand he bounded up to Sally's office on the third floor.

Jenny was busy with the morning's mail as Ray breezed passed her shouting good morning and almost danced into Sally's office.

"How's my favorite Insurance agent?" he gushed as he kissed Sally on the cheek.

"Well what do I owe this honor?" she said, ignoring his question.

"Just couldn't wait for tonight!" He jibed

"I don't believe that for one minute," she scolded looking quizzically at him

Since the successful Internet project they both worked on years ago Sally had grown both in maturity and status within Global and was now a Director of Operations. The department she headed was charged with introducing new practices and procedures anywhere within the company to make Global Insurance more efficient. The department had had many titles ranging from Organization and Methods in the 60's through Operations Research in the 70's and finally re-engineering in the 90's. But the bottom line was the relentless pursuit of efficiency and as such Sally had access to many of Global's inner workings.

"Well there could be an ulterior motive for the visit!" mused Ray, "but I've lost it now that I've seen you! Where's the coffee?" Ray knew that curiosity would overcome Sally and decided to move slowly to tease her.

"Let's not fence eh" she grated "And you know where the coffee is!"

Ray feigned a hurt look and backed out of the office in the direction of the coffeepot. "Want a cup?" he asked.

"No!" she said firmly and pretended to organize her desk, then sat down to read some old memos. He returned shortly and sat down in front of her desk quietly sipping the hot coffee intently.

"Well!" she demanded "What's this all about?"

"What do you know about Global Bank, Ltd?" he started.

"Not much!" she said "Subsidiary of Insurance Inc. purpose is to move funds internationally mainly through tax havens, some say it's the core strength of the whole company... why do you want to know?" she asked.

"I came across some message earlier today where they seemed to be transferring large sums of money throughout Asia on a strange timetable!" Ray alluded.

Sally's interest peeked to say the least, she sat alert.

Ray continued, "The message sent by someone named PAT who confirmed the transfer of ninety nine million dollars from New Zealand to Australia at five minutes before midnight," Ray sipped his coffee again.

"Both the amount and timing looked odd," he added.

Sally agreed on the timing point, but countered that the amount could just be the clearing of a particular account, which happened to be ninety nine million dollars.

"Then the message continued that the next transfer was to occur from Australia to Hong Kong again five minutes before midnight."

Sally sat upright; this had just become intriguing. "How come the CIA is monitoring our internal networks?" Sally asked with a legal intonation.

"That's just it!" Raymond said, "this was over normal radio frequencies, not telephone or E-mail, but high powered radios."

Sally could not rationalize any of this and was lost in thought.

"Who would this PAT person be?" Interrupted Raymond.

"I have no idea, but let's see what I can dig up," she turned to her computer screen and punched in the various instructions prompted by the screen, eventually three names appeared.

Name	Occupation
Patrick Hugo	Sales Rep
Patrick Kelly	I.S. Manager

Patricia Knoll   clerk"

"Well the voice definitely sounded male!" Raymond informed Sally, "so there are two possibilities, and I doubt whether a sales rep would be around at midnight New Year's eve," he offered.

"Sounds logical to me!" Sally agreed, "Lets concentrate on Mr. Kelly."

"Any data on him?"

Sally punched in more instructions and the computer screen yielded its data.

"Patrick Kelly, Manager, Information systems.

Employment date - May 1, 1996

Date of Birth - June 16, 1975

Address: 16 Dock Road, Apt.1A, Bondi, NSW

Comments: Adequate performer, however no ambition to advance."

"Nothing startling here!" Sally volunteered, "But he seems to be the only PAT capable of transferring ninety nine million dollars electronically."

Raymond queried the ninety nine million dollars and Sally punched more instructions into the system, this time querying Global Banks' policies and procedures. Sally's eyes caught the relevant phrase immediately.

"In New Zealand's manual Section 9, Paragraph

3G   Balances up to $99 million can be transferred to other Global Bank Accounts with local approval only.

3H   Balances between $100 million and $250 million require Regional approval."

The relevance of $99 million became clear, but the reason still evaded them. Sally sat back trying to make sense out of a transaction which had not really broken any company rules; however, she felt increasingly uncomfortable about it. She also did not like the fact that Raymond, the CIA, also knew about it. They sat in silence not daring to interrupt each other's thoughts.

Finally Sally thought aloud. "Even if this was an illegal act surely the audit trail would be left by electronic authorizations."

Raymond's eyes glinted and he blurted out. "Not if the systems and networks are in chaos after midnight."

"What do you mean?" inquired Sally?"

"Well remember the millennium bug or Y2K problem that all IS departments were working frantically at some years ago?"

"Yes," Sally looked perplexed.

"Well it's time to see if it all worked and my bet is it probably didn't!" Raymond stated emphatically, and drained his coffee.

"We've had sporadic reports indicating system problems over in Asia since midnight. Nothing overwhelmingly catastrophic as yet confirmed, but a series of events only explained by the possible breakdown of control systems."

Sally sat mesmerized. She was not ready for the consequences of her thoughts. She seemed to be in a dream trying to swim to the end of her consciousness and return to reality. Nothing broke this mystical world between disbelief and despair.

"Two things could be happening here!" Raymond's voice boomed and echoed in the canyons of her thoughts. "One, the company could be protecting its cash by moving it at the last minute or two, there is an illegal transaction being made. If it's illegal, the "Millennium Bug" may wipe out all trace of the transaction. The perpetrators could even have planted a virus which would have the same effect."

Sally fought to collect her scattered thoughts. "The consequences of Raymond's comments on Global Insurance were bad enough, but what could the world wake up to tomorrow?"

"What can we do?" she asked hesitantly.

"We must confirm our suspicions about Global, which we can then use to get a credible story together before we involve any other people either inside or outside of the company."

"How do we do that?" Sally inquired worrying about exposing this Achilles like vulnerability.

Raymond was firing on all eight cylinders now. "Can you work out the likely transfer path of a series of transactions and possible final destinations, knowing what you know about Global's policies and procedures?" He rubbed his chin thoughtfully. "Also any known associates of Pat Kelly. I'll try to get someone to check out the Sydney and Hong Kong end!"

Sally affirmed that she could do this and Raymond took down the details about Patrick Kelly, which still remained on Sally's computer screen. With that he leaned over and kissed Sally, giving her a reassuring wink, he then left her office shouting that he would call her in about an hour. Jenny watched as Raymond dodged several people in the corridor before colliding with the mail clerk and disappearing into the elevator, looking a bit flustered.

He was lost in thought as he gunned the Cadillac back to his office and really had no idea how he avoided an accident as the last thing on his mind was driving, the only thing he remembered was that the traffic lights were all in his favor.

After a short visit to his office he burst into the communications office and asked if they could connect him to Jon David on this frequency, and thrust it in front of the most junior operator. The time passed torturously slow as the connection was tried and tried again. Raymond was just about to give up when a groggy Jon answered his radio set

"Yeah! Jon here!" crackled and broke Raymond's concentration.

"Jon, this is Raymond Bennett a friend of Tom Ricer's I work for the U.S. Government in Washington."

"Oh, what can I do for you?" Jon sounded more alert.

"I was talking to Tom earlier and he told me about your explanation of the unexplained events over there."

Jon became a little tentative, but Raymond continued.

"I think you are right." He paused for effect, "I have come across some other incidents which also confirm your ideas."

Jon was all attention now.

"You remember the transfer of money that Tom mentioned?" Raymond asked as he vaguely remembered the results of a 1998 survey stating that 38% of Information Technology people would withdraw their funds from banks and investment companies in preparation of the Y2K failure. " It seemed ludicrous that an Insurance company was doing just that," he thought.

"Yea, but I never read anything into it!" Jon replied.

Raymond then went through the main points of the transaction with Jon who still remained skeptical of his conclusion.

"It just doesn't make sense!" Raymond concluded.

"What would really help is if we could find a link between Pat Kelly and any others involved to at least confirm or verify that there is something up."

Jon could not follow Raymond's drift.

"What do you want me to do?" he asked sharply.

"Pat Kelly, like you, lives near Sydney," Raymond stated. "If you could visit him or ask neighbors it might help, I don't know any other way."

"Why don't you ask via official connections?" Jon came back.

"I've tried and it would take too long," was the short reply. There was a long pause while Jon thought about it.

"O.K., O.K." Jon relented, "I'll see what I can do, what's the address?"

Raymond gave Jon the address and signed off.

CHAPTER 11

Jon was still skeptical about Raymond's theory but hell; he had nothing better to do. He showered and changed his clothes and took two more Panadols to shake off his headache. Chugging down a half-pint of orange juice to chase the dehydration away.

He rolled his 1962 Norton Dominator 99 motor cycle out of the garden shed and pushed it out to the road. His face showed the pride of ownership of one of the noblest names in motorcycling history, the "unapproachable Norton" he murmured to himself.

It was too early to fire up the 597 cc engine near the house on this New Year's Day and Jon was feeling unusually charitable for some reason, or perhaps it was the beginning of stealth creeping into his psyche as he prepared to spy on this Pat Kelly.

He wheeled the bike about one hundred feet from the front of his apartment building, then switched on the ignition. The bike roared into life at the first kick, and he kept the twin cylinder engine revs, at three thousand to warm it up quickly while he looked at the address he had jotted down on the corner of a newspaper. John had no idea what he was going to do once he got to where he was going and hoped the ride would give him the much needed inspiration. He followed the coast road, noting the odd luminescence of the breaking waves as light refracted from the orange ball half way over the horizon.

Although the bike was capable of one hundred miles per hour he kept his speed down to forty-five. The roads were unusually quiet and he noted that the traffic lights were still not working, making him extra vigilant at crossroads. The powerful engine purred softly and the rush of warm air did invigorate him, but inspiration was still lagging. After a twenty-minute ride he approached the vicinity of Dock Road and cruised up and down the tight parallel streets, until he located the target street and then the house. Number 16 was a row house built of brick with upper and lower apartments, 1a was the lower one, with a red painted door framed in white. Jon sat at the south end of the street staring at the apartment still waiting for inspiration when he decided to look around the rear of the house. He walked about one hundred yards to a cross street, which took him to a back lane running parallel to the houses.

The backs of these houses were all alike with only different color paint work to distinguish them, all looked quiet at number 1a, with the rear of the house as nondescript as the front. Jon noted that the small rear yard with a five-foot wall afforded more cover to get a closer look inside than the front of the house.

He returned to the front again, looking for some reason to approach the house when he noticed the front door opening. Out strode a young man; Jon guessed that he was in his late twenties, he was about five feet eleven and had long stringy dark hair, which needed combing. His appearance was disheveled, as if he had just woken up from a rough night or had been working all night. He needed a shave badly. He ran his fingers through his hair and walked away from him in a slow unpurposeful way. He wore a dark green polo shirt with a dark jacket and gray trousers, all badly needed pressing. His whole appearance looked like a throwback from the sixties with unkempt hair that hid a pointed face and shifty brown eyes.

Jon watched him saunter up Dock Street, turn left at a cross street and disappear. He decided to take a chance, and quickly retraced his steps to the rear of the apartment, passed through the small yard and looked into what seemed to be a bedroom. It was a mess with clothes strewn all over the place but nothing suspicious jumped out at him. The window was partly open, so he pushed it upward slightly to his surprise it moved easily. He looked around and seeing no obvious danger impulsively dove through the opening, crashing silently into a pile of shoes and clothes. He raised himself up on one knee listening for any perceptible noise, but all was quiet. Looking around the room he noted the bland cream wallpaper, and white paint, his reflection stared back at him from the mirror of an old pre-war oak dresser, the single modern pine bedside table made for an eclectic look. He looked at the clothes strewn over the floor and he noticed both male and female items, but nothing caught his attention and he moved to the door. He slowly looked out into a passageway. To his right he saw the front door, and what he thought would be the main room of the apartment. To his left and the rear of the house it, he saw the kitchen and beyond that a small bathroom.

He moved slowly out into the passageway, his heart working overtime-pumping blood to all his senses, which were near screaming point now. The floor creaked and at the same time he thought he heard a sound behind him, coming from the kitchen. He stood still, straining to hear, something moved above him, a chair scraping across the floor, lessened the tension momentarily. He sighed with relief and gingerly moved on and into the front room.

Again an untidy mess greeted him. He glanced around and noticed at once the HF radio sitting on an old oak coffee table in the left-hand corner of the room. Jon quickly padded over to the set and scanned the debris on the table. It contained hand written notes intermingled with printed instructions and what looked to be computer manuals. To his left he saw a laptop computer lying on the floor still hooked up to the telephone jack the screen saver constantly changing images of the Irish flag. Like the bedroom, this room was scantily furnished with an old heavy sofa fronted by a pine coffee table acting as the focal point of the room. There were two wing chairs with side tables and an inexpensive eight-foot by twelve-foot rug on the floor. The bay window had a chest for decoration, over which draped a small Irish flag. Several of the tables had what looked like old family pictures sitting peering out into the room.

Suddenly the radio crackled and startled him, his muscles tensed and instinctively he lurched forward and scrambled to turn the volume down. Silence re-entered the room; he stared at the set momentarily, then bent over and removed the fuse from the rear of the set, to disable it. His brow beaded with perspiration and he felt flushed. Taking a deep breath he glanced toward the door fearful that someone had heard him. Nothing stirred so he looked down at the table and noticed a series of scribbles on a writing pad. He picked it up for a closer look, recognizing some of the figures as frequencies and unconsciously pushed them into his pocket, the others had various shorthand notes, which he could not decipher.

His concentration was disturbed when again he heard a noise. This time it was not from upstairs. His brow was beaded with sweat, his legs felt weak as if his body were too heavy for them. Not realizing he was moving, he stumbled over a pile of old newspapers and fell on one knee to the floor. He clenched his teeth in pain and looked disdainfully at the old headline.

"British/Irish Peace talks break down, little hope seen!"

"Patrick, you back already?" The question came from the passageway and belonged to a female with an Irish accent.

Jon was paralyzed, he stuffed the paper notes he was carrying, into his other jean pocket and dodged behind the opening door. He was too slow and the door caught him in mid flight. A young woman appeared, wrapped only in a towel. She saw him and instinctively let out a loud scream. Jon lunged at her and firmly clamped his hand over her mouth. He wrapped his other arm around her waist and held onto her tightly. She squirmed and bit his hand, he cursed but managed to hold on to her, the towel dropped to the floor, leaving her naked. He lost his grip and she turned her head to look at him squarely, her large green eyes, momentarily clouded with fear became filled with hatred. She had a hard look about her and her flushed cheeks gave her a wild appearance.

"You son of a bitch," she spat at him and twisted away from him. She began to kick out at him. Jon held on to her anyway he could and found the ensuing wrestling match strangely erotic and felt himself becoming aroused. He was holding her from behind now with his left hand over her mouth and his right arm in a strangle hold, around her neck, he tried to keep his balance. He frog marched her back through the kitchen and then into the bathroom. They could hardly move in the confined space. He ripped a towel from a holder and put it over her head both to disorientate her and to prevent further recognition, knowing that this was fruitless. Keeping her in a strangle hold, he grabbed her tights which were on the bathroom floor. He then used his knees to force her off balance and pushed her face down between the wall and the bathtub side, his weight kept her lodged. He quickly wrapped the tights around one wrist and then tied the other wrist. She could hardly move now and was breathing heavily.

"Bastard! You'll pay for this!" he heard her gasp.

His eyes scoured the bathroom and he managed to reach for a small curtain, which limply hung from the window. His breathing was labored, as he wrapped this around her ankles, then tied it loosely around the tights on her wrists, the knots were not very good but they would disable her long enough for him to disappear. He left her face downward cursing madly with a towel loosely around her head, hands tied behind her back and her legs bent and tied to her wrists. Jon dived down the corridor and out the front door and charged towards his bike. "Thank God I left the bike pointing in the right direction" he thought as he grabbed the handlebars and pushed the bike down Dock Road. Jump starting the old Norton he sped for home with a huge laugh welling up inside of him at the bizarre events of the last five minutes.

He reached home in about twenty minutes, left his bike on the street, and ran to his kitchen where he chugged a long drink of orange juice straight from the carton. His throat had been parched with the tension and his heart was still beating wildly, yet he felt strangely exhilarated and even turned on by the last hour's experience.

He sat down and found a glass to pour the remaining orange juice in and slowly sipped it, as he searched in his pockets for the stolen notes.

There were three notes, written on yellow paper, one definitely depicted radio frequencies and times, another included a list of digits in code like format and the last was something written in a foreign language, which looked slightly familiar yet which made no sense to him. He laid them out on the kitchen table but after five minutes of staring at them was still none-the wiser. Tiredness washed over him and he went to lie down, he glanced at the radio and decided to call Raymond and pass the contents of the notes to him. It took about ten minutes for him to reach Raymond, who sounded tired and anxious.

Jon laughed to himself as he recalled his small adventure to Raymond and then relayed the contents of the three notes. The first, both Raymond and Jon agreed, were radio frequencies and the fact that Pat Kelly had the radio at home raised both their suspicions. The second note, Raymond thought, looked like a series of bank accounts, however, the third note drew a blank with them both.

"I'll try and get this checked out and get back to you," Raymond volunteered.

"Tom told me you were a computer genius! How did you figure out the year 2000 problems?"

"Coincidence really," Jon said, matter of fact I had done some programming years ago and remembered the issue but always thought that Governments and corporations would either beat the deadline or broadcast the consequences before anything happened. I tried my credit card today and the system closed down. When looking at the expiration date 2001, it triggered the answer. Two thousand and one, the movie lives," he joked.

"I still don't believe we left so many loose ends," he mused.

Raymond said that he was still receiving sporadic reports of incidents but no one is admitting to a universal problem as yet.

"I think most organizations will still be in denial, disbelief or just plain ignorant of the pervasiveness of the problem, Millie will have her way!" Jon said flatly.

Raymond signed off and faxed the bank account numbers over to Sally who went to work on them.

The radio frequencies, he sent to Terry Frazier, a communications specialist, to see if he could shed any light on them and the third note he did not know what to do with immediately. He walked out of his office for a coffee and decided to ask Bill Drummond for his opinion.

"Still here?" he growled. Can't get enough excitement at home?"

Raymond remembered he was now in his 11th hour at work and felt like it. He put a copy of the third note in front of Bill and said, "What do you make of this?"

Bill studied it but just could not grasp what language it was, he was at a complete loss, seemingly recognizing some words but not the whole note which really perplexed him and wondered if it were in code.

"Let's send it to the code experts," he suggested.

Raymond was reluctant, as he did not really know if it was anything relevant but his gut told him it was important. "I'll walk it over, who should I go to?"

Bill immediately said, "Victor Gomez is the guy to see, I'll call and see if he's in."

Two minutes later Raymond was in the elevator to the tenth floor to see Victor thanks again to Bill Drummond. Victor looked at the note and rubbed his goatee beard studiously

"Hm," he murmured. "Nothing jumps out immediately but lets put it into our box of tricks."

He walked over to a piece of equipment which looked like a photocopier but had the famous hp logo prominently displayed denoting Hewlett Packard technology lay behind the gray plastic facade. Victor scanned in the note and keyed in some commands. One minute later not only did Raymond know what language or code it was but had the translation into English also.

Victor read the screen to Raymond. "The language is Gaelic an ancient language from the British Isles. Mainly used by the Irish, Welsh and Scottish nationalist people. This particular version seems to be Irish."

The translation read. "Arrange for transfers to be in MAUI by New Years Eve. Hawaii time!"

Victor pressed the print key and the contents of the screen appeared in hard copy. Raymond could hardly believe it.

Victor smiled "The system comes through again, what would you do without us back room boys?"

Raymond was impressed but could not resist a departing jibe. "Enjoy it while you can, it may not be functioning tomorrow," and left a perplexed Victor Gomez.

"Thanks again," he shouted from the corridor.

Victor stared at the equipment with a quizzical look on his face, and stroked his beard idly. "Wonder what he is on?" he shook his head and smiled.

CHAPTER 12

Raymond had enough now to involve his director, Albert Pagano, something he did not relish.

Albert Pagano was a lifelong CIA professional who knew all the internal ropes; he was not well liked either by the administration staff or the field operatives who did not trust him. He had been described as shady but some people viewed the description as a compliment.

He was about 5-ft. 6-ins. tall with sharp features, ginger blonde hair and piercingly mole like eyes, which avoided maintaining eye contact with anyone very long and therefore came across as shifty. No one could understand how he had progressed up the ranks, as he was never credited with doing anything. He always spouted the new buzzwords and supported initiatives that were close to success but real risk was unknown to him, as was loyalty. If something was going wrong which involved him he always managed to distance himself from the problem and became known as "Teflon Al." The popular theory was that he must have some dirt on his superiors, but this was never substantiated.

Raymond called Albert Pagano's secretary for an urgent appointment. It was not often that the two men met at

Raymond's request, in fact this would only be the second time, so Raymond was not surprised that he had to wait some minutes before Pagano came on the line.

"What can I do for you Raymond?" he said cordially.

"Well Sir, I have come across some disturbing data about which you should be aware!" Raymond stated coolly.

"What is it in connection with?" Pagano asked.

"An unusual money transfer and possible robbery involving a U.S. company."

"Then you'd better come up immediately!" Pagano ordered rather than requested.

"Yes sir!" Raymond signed off.

Pagano's office was on the fourteenth floor, actually it was the thirteenth, but superstition still prevailed. Raymond always had an uncomfortable feeling on this floor but could not discern if it was the place itself, or that he never had considered thirteen lucky. He wove his way up to this boss's office and prepared to wait the mandatory wait that all underlings experienced in large corporations. The CIA was no different when it came to status and egos; Surprisingly Raymond was shown straight in.

"Sit down Raymond." Pagano gestured towards a chair in front of his desk. He smiled a measured smile, polite not friendly. "Your message just now sounded very intriguing, I must say," Pagano continued. "Please continue with your story." His beady black eyes were like lasers. He leaned back in his oversized chair and placed his hands, prayer like, in front of him.

Raymond was a little taken aback by the speed with which he was in front of Pagano fully expecting to rehearse his story several times while waiting, he scrambled for the starting point and began to relay today's events. "At about 7:30 a.m. today I received a series of unrelated reports involving incidents occurring around midnight commencing in New Zealand. These incidents involved unconfirmed accidents involving aircraft, shipping; trains and even an overflowing dam. I spoke with someone in Australia to verify whether or not he had any knowledge of these accidents; he confirmed them!" Raymond paused, his lips parted but no sounds came.

Pagano had been quiet until now, "Could these incidents be related? he asked, his eyelids narrowed.

Raymond swallowed hard, he had hoped to mention the terrorist threat before bringing in the technological mysteries of the year 2,000 to the limelight. "Well Sir, Er .." Raymond sounded flustered. "All these events seemed to have occurred around midnight, local time and as you know this, is also the change of the millennium."

"Yes!" Pagano nodded, his forehead wrinkled.

"Computerized systems and controls find the year 2,000 a discontinuity from the previous years because of a programming quirk well known by programmers for over thirty years."

"Yes" Pagano replied, "I am aware of the problem, but billions of dollars had been spent on remedying this," he claimed, authoritatively. "The CIA itself has spent over four hundred million dollars on the project," he added. He began tapping his fingertips together now, impatience settling in.

"Yes Sir", continued Raymond, "But not all companies and agencies have been as prudent as we have. Any shortcut taken or date correction missed could cause problems and I'm afraid we are experiencing sporadic problems involving this "Millennium Bug" as it is known." Raymond swallowed hard. "It has been constantly forecast that twenty percent of systems will not be ready in time," Raymond blurted out, his confidence fading.

Pagano had heard this before but did not really give any credance to it. The skeptics always thought the technological technological experts were hyping the problem to the extreme to gain either money or publicity, or both," he stated flatly. "I'm not sure you have got anything-new here Raymond." Pagano rasped the edge to his voice indicating some frustration, his face stiffened.

Raymond battled on ... "During the course of investigating these events our contact in the Pacific came across an unusual message indicating a large transfer of money, This transaction occurred just before midnight local time, and involved the Global Insurance Co., Routine inquiries yielded suspicious circumstances and Global is currently investigating the transfer themselves." Raymond was exhausted and beginning to doubt if his deductions were right after all. "However during a follow up on these transactions they appeared to be linked with some arms deal being arranged by the IRA, or the ILA." Raymond flushed; he was in over his head now and wished he had checked in with Sally regarding the list of bank accounts before making the last statement. He shuffled uncomfortably in the chair.

Pagano's eyes widened at the mention of the I.L.A. and he tapped his fingers idly on the desk top

Raymond sensed some progress here and pressed. "As you know the Irish peace talks have broken down and the ILA are furious that popular opinion forced them to disarm."

These facts had been published in every European paper and so were irrefutable and gave some credence to Raymond's deduction that something could be happening.

"Why do you think that the financial transactions and the other incidents are linked," Pagano inquired.

"Only that the illegal transfer of money will be impossible to track through the networks after midnight because of the systems problem, Maui was mentioned and the "Kingfisher," a known gun runner is in Hawaiian waters."

Pagano was uneasy, he sensed that he was in risky territory. Not one explanation presented was concrete however the total picture held some credibility.

Raymond sensed Pagano's indecision and placed a copy of the Gaelic note and translation in front of him, saying that this was obtained at the site of the first transfer of money.

Pagano looked hard at the note. "How did you get this?" he inquired.

"One of our operatives," Raymond murmured quietly as if afraid to be heard. He was way in over his head now and began to sweat.

"Leave this with me for now!" Pagano said, with a tone of finality in his voice. "I'll make some inquiries he added," as an after thought.

Raymond stood up stiffly, turned and made for the door with mixed feelings. He was relieved that the meeting was all over but concerned that nothing would happen. Pagano had looked really uneasy and unlikely to proceed with it further unless more evidence could be supplied.

Raymond desperately needed to get in touch with Sally, impatience welling up inside of him as he waited for the elevator to take him back to his office.

Pagano sat deep in thought and unconsciously stroked his chin. He went over the points of the meeting and mentally complemented Raymond Bennett for his alertness and astuteness in putting these events together, but it was still incomplete, too risky to escalate at the moment.

He had to talk to one of his peers as soon as possible.

Raymond dove into his office; all fingers and thumbs as he dialed Sally's number

"Damn it! Wrong number," he spat. and punched the keys again.

Finally Jenny's voice came on the line "Certainly she'll speak with you," she said, when Raymond asked and put him through.

Both Sally and Raymond began to talk at once then both excused themselves.

Sally was first and she related her last forty-five minutes since they had spoken. "Yes the list of bank accounts were all Global's except one. No, the transactions could not be confirmed as the network was down in Asia Pacific for some unknown reason!" she sounded hopeful yet unconvincing, " but it is a holiday and a weekend." She added. "No one in head office knew about any projected major transfers of money after hours."

The words hung in the air waiting to be absorbed. This was dynamite news and both felt the rush of excitement flood over them like a crashing wave pulling them ever deeper into a global mystery. It felt unreal, like a dream.

Now it was Raymond's turn and he related his story about talking to Bill Pagano and emphasized the translation of the Gaelic note. Then Raymond hit his head with the palm of his hand. He just remembered that he left the frequency information with Terry Frazier in communications. "Sally I've got to go; I'll call you soon." He slammed down the receiver then picked it up immediately and punched out Terry's number.

"Terry Frazier speaking!" The Scottish accent was thick.

"Terry, this is Raymond Bennett, any news on those frequencies and call addresses?"

"Yeah, the frequencies are nothing special, no restrictions, secret code, or any such nonsense, and there is nothing special about the addresses, which are based in Sydney, Hong Kong,

Singapore, Zurich, Jersey, London, Boston, Dublin and Lahaina." He cleared his throat the excused himself. "I checked the Boston Radio license, it belongs to a guy called John McKenzie, his address is…"

Raymond jotted down the details unconsciously. He felt dejected, no real lead here. The balloon of knowledge seemed to deflate visibly in his mind.

"Thanks Terry," Raymond said dejectedly, "owe you one." He returned the receiver slowly to the phone on his desk, the adrenaline seemed to drain from him, he felt sure those addresses were important.

Raymond suddenly felt tired; the hours and excitement were catching up with him. He needed a break and a sweet coffee to increase his blood sugar. He made his way to the cafeteria and collected a large coffee and Danish from the self-service racks. He mechanically paid a subsidized $2.15 to the cashier and found a quiet table to devour his breakfast. The fifteen-minute break did him the world of good and he felt better as he made his way back to his office. He called Sally again, getting her direct this time.

She asked about the radio information and sensed Raymond's disappointment as he listed the city's which were involved.

"Strange!" Sally said after she looked at the list she had copied.

"What?" Raymond asked.

"These cities are the same as the list of bank accounts you gave me, all except the last one Lahaina."

"Strange indeed!" repeated Raymond "Where is Lahaina anyway, sounds Spanish to me?" he added.

"Yes it does sound Spanish or French!" Sally said, "and we do have a large company in both countries, but not there….Wait!" Sally, shouted as she jumped up.

Raymond heard the receiver clash to the desk and heard Sally and Jenny talking in the background.

"I've asked Jenny to check with our travel agency about Lahaina!" Sally returned. She carried the conversation for the two minutes it took Jenny to find out where this strange town was. Raymond heard Jenny tease Sally

"So you're going for a romantic time in Hawaii are you?"

Sally relayed the news to Raymond and confirmed that Lahaina was on Maui in the Hawaiian Islands, "No connection to Global." She added.

Raymond mentally pictured Maui and found himself fingering the notes he had taken down from Jon in Australia. There in the Gaelic note was clearly Maui.. Raymond's mind put another piece of the jigsaw together; the final destination for Global's money was Maui. "Jesus Christ," he exhaled, "That's it!" his voice almost broke. "Lahaina, must be pivotal in this whole thing."

"We now have the time, and the place, but who is behind it all?" Sally thought out loud.

"If we knew that you would call me Sherlock Holmes!" Raymond smiled. "The only name we came across was a guy called John McKenzie who owns a radio in Boston!"

Sally could not believe her ears. "Who?" she shouted into the mouthpiece "Who did you say?"

"John McKenzie!" Raymond sensed Sally's excitement.

"McKenzie!" Sally shouted, "McKenzie is the person who hired Kelly!" The words gushed out over the telephone line.

CHAPTER 13

Al Pagano watched Raymond leave his office and remained deep in thought about how or even if, he should proceed. His immediate thought was to contact his counterpart in the Defense Intelligence Agency, Dave Prezzano. The DIA specialized in counter terrorism activities and would presumably know of any illegal armament activity.

He asked his secretary to call Prezzano's number seriously doubting if he would be in today. Pagano leaned back in his chair, he felt comfortable asking for Prezzano's advice and he hoped he could talk with him. As he thought, Prezzano had taken a vacation probably on the assumption that the terrorists would also. He asked his secretary to then contact Prezzano's deputy, Michael Carey. Carey was out of the office, but his assistant said he would return the call as soon as possible.

It was about ten minutes later that an intrigued Michael Carey asked how he could help Mr. Pagano, apologizing for the delay first. The two people had barely met before so the attempt at small talk was awkward for both and they got to the reason for the call quickly.

Pagano began by qualifying the need for this inquiry almost

degrading it to a nuisance status. This was to hedge his bets and not raise any false alarms. He got to the meat of the matter saying that one of his assistants had come across the vague possibility of an arms deal in some harmless reports. "There is probably nothing in this but I thought I would check with you!" Pagano ended.

Carey listened intently. It was not often he had the opportunity to impress the director of another Agency and was more than willing to cooperate thinking that it couldn't hurt so long as he did not compromise Prezzano's position.

Prezzano's Group monitored activity relating to the movement of known and suspected terrorists, arms, military type vehicles and parts, and other related commodities. Trouble could be predicted well in advance by collating the deliveries of many varying and seeming unrelated products, for instance, a sudden large shipment of burns treatment or severe painkillers from pharmaceutical companies might predict an outbreak or escalation of violence or even war as had happened with the six day war between Israel and Egypt. Intelligence about ship's cargoes and movements were monitored on a regular basis and Prezanno's group used all the techniques available to predict trouble

Carey was aware of several potential arms deals involving both the usual and some new players, but did not immediately volunteer the information. With the breakdown of the USSR multiple sources of arms had developed and there was always customers. Even after the Gulf War, Iraq had continued to buy arms primarily via a Bosnian connection. The historically based conflicts throughout the world always represented an opportunity for someone. Current sources of arms included the Ukraine, Russia, Pakistan, India, Columbia, and even Israel who all need valuable foreign currencies, particularly US dollars.

About three months ago, Britain's MI6 had passed to the CIA details of a concentration of arms' exports, potentially to Central

America. This was the only recent larger scale transaction and the theory was a potential drug related war was imminent. The ship Kingfisher was suspected to be shipping the arms from India across the pacific, to Tumaco, Columbia. Carey passed this information to Pagano; comfortable that Prezzano would approve. It was relatively old data and there would be no political fallout if the information leaked.

Pagano thanked Carey for his assistance and signed off, wishing him a happy New Year. He sat focussing on the recently cradled telephone as if it were going to provide the next step for him to take. Staring with unfocussed eyes Pagano still was not convinced that Raymond's theory was valid but also recognized that another piece of the puzzle may have been put to place. The phone rang and startled him out of his preoccupation.

"Raymond Bennett on the line Sir," His secretary informed him.

"Hello Raymond!" Pagano ventured.

"Hello sir!" I just wanted to update you with the latest, Raymond said tentatively.

"Go ahead!" Pagano leaned back in his chair and put him on speaker.

"Since we met," Raymond went on "I have had confirmation that all the bank accounts on the note were identified as Global's, except one. This last one is situated in Lahaina, on Maui. This Hawiian bank account seems to be the final link in the transfer of the large sums of money across the globe. These transfers are a mystery to Global's management here in the U.S.A., Sir?" Raymond hesitated, "I think we've stumbled on something here!"

"Hmm," murmured Pagano, "I think you may be right, I'm going to contact the Executive Director, I'll get back to you." He cradled the phone and sat back in his chair. Pagano was reticent to contact the Executive Director of the CIA, John J. Sloan, especially on a semi-holiday. An image of him flashed in his minds eye.

Sloan was a dynamo of a man; about 6'2" tall. His bearing and speech conveyed both intelligence and competence; he had black curly hair, brown eyes, which challenged the world, and a broad expressive mouth. He had started out in life as an entrepreneur and made a fortune in security and surveillance systems in the 1960's when everyone was paranoid about the cold war. His charismatic personality and vast knowledge of the security industry made him a natural to serve on various governmental advisory committees. He became well liked by members of both Republican and Democratic parties and was known for his candid opinions and free advice. Collecting vast sums of money did not motivate John J. Sloan, so when he was approached about the possibility of joining the CIA as director of National Security NSA, he jumped at the chance. He sold his business to a competitor and John dedicated the next five years to the government. The first three years flew by as his pragmatic approach brought many changes to NSA after which he was promoted to the Executive Director of the CIA. In this role, he reported to the Director of Central Intelligence, George Trent, who was accountable to the president and Congress. John was considered an approachable person and he valued teamwork and co-operation both within the CIA and with other agencies, however patience was not his strong suit, so any interface with him had to be accurate and concise.

Pagano picked up the phone and dialed Sloan's number. The phone rang once and transferred directly to voice mail. Sloan's commanding voice informed the listener of his unavailability and gave three telephone numbers where he could be reached.

Pagano was relieved. However, this relief was short lived as he began dialing the other numbers. Sloan was on the line with Pagano's second attempt and, after an apologetic start for disturbing him Pagano soon relayed the days events.

Sloan was an intuitive man and grasped the seriousness of the situation immediately. His decision-making ability was what disturbed his direct reports most; he reacted like a machine gun giving quick-fired instructions on what to do next.

His exact instructions were lost somewhere in the phone lines, but Pagano's own version of short hand captured most of it.

The result of this five-minute conversation was a meeting with the President in one hour, which Sloan would arrange. Pagano's responsibilities were to assemble the relevant people including Global's executives and the FBI director, Hank Woodward. All must attend even if it was via teleconference.

REALIZATION

CHAPTER 14

Somewhere in the White House a clock chimed 10:00 a.m. as the small group of people assembled in the Oval Office, welcomed by Vice President Alex Scott. President Alexander was due to arrive in about five minutes. The assembly comprised of Al Scott, John Sloan, Hank Woodward and Mike Carey together with Raymond and Sally who were sitting together quietly looking around this famous office in awe. Their stomachs were in knots, their mouths parched, and both were sure their legs would give way if they had to stand up. Raymond now regretted not making a second trip to the bathroom, which only exacerbated his discomfort. Scott, Sloan, and Woodward were making small talk beside the President's desk. Pagano and Carey huddled around Sally and Raymond to discuss last minute details. Art Gregory, the Chairman and the CEO of Global Insurance Inc. and Dave Prezzano would teleconference in; a White House communications officer was on hand to facilitate this.

The atmosphere tensed in anticipation of the President's entrance, which seemed to be on queue. Alexander strode in purposefully offering a "Good morning to all." Those seated rose as a sign of respect. He smiled and thanked his guests for coming on such an important day. This cordial gesture was designed to diffuse the tension and apprehension, which pervaded the room. He stood in front of his desk and leaning backwards, took some of the weight off his legs. The telecommunication expert verified the teleconference attendees, nodded to the President and left the office, quietly closing the door behind him.

President Alexander was a little less than six foot tall; he made his presence felt as he glanced around the oval office with dark intimidating eyes. Nodding slightly at the group, he sat on the edge of the desk and casually ran his right hand through his thinning gray hair. He was ruggedly handsome; his wide nose was in proportion with his square jawed face. His smile revealed a perfect set of teeth framed by wide full lips. He started the proceedings by asking everyone to introduce themselves; this took up the first six minutes and made everyone feel a little more comfortable. Art Gregory, Global's Chairman was the last person to speak, the telephone line went quiet and a brief awkward silence ensued before Sloan requested Raymond to briefly summarize the situation.

During his prologue Raymond paused for input from Sally and Pagano, who both verified his story adding supporting thoughts when appropriate. The audience listened without interruption, occasionally looking at one another uncomfortably and all trying to avoid the President's cold stare when the briefing was complete. Alexander slowly looked around the group, still leaning against the desk; he seemed lost in thought and rested his chin against his chest for a moment. He then stiffened and stood up from the desk, and looked at the group somewhat sternly.

"Gentlemen!" the President started, "If I read the situation correctly, we have two separate, but potentially serious situations here! The first; a redirection of funds from one of America's premier companies, Global Insurance, possibly linked to terrorist activities and secondly," he paused, looking grave. "The potential chaotic, if not catastrophic impact due to computer system failures because of their non-compliance with the year 2,000 date!"

Various sounds of agreement echoed throughout the office, when he paused again. Several people took the opportunity to clear their throats.

"Let's take the "Bug Thing" first!" Alexander continued. He talked into the speakerphone addressing Art Gregory.

"Art! What is your perspective of this millennium bug issue?"

Art coughed, uncomfortably, excused himself then began to answer; the tinny sound invaded the oval office.

"Mr. President we...we've been working on this issue for five years or more and have spent over nine hundred million dollars. We are confident that we have solved most of our problems, however our experts now tell me that our main systems are still vulnerable on several counts. One, imported data from external sources – If defective data is transferred to our compliant systems from external sources there still may be a serious problem." He coughed again, his throat was dry. "This will be something like current virus attacks, which spread like wildfire if not detected. The only problem now is we will have no detection software to warn us or correct the problem." Art did not sound confident.

"How likely is this?" The President again, sounding surprisingly firm.

"We don't really know but let us guess at a five percent incidence!" Art stated coolly, without the benefit of any real evidence that the figure was correct.

"Two, imported data from internal sources, for example, individual PCs may still have uncorrected dates in their systems. If interfaced with our main systems inadvertently, problems will be experienced. Every individual P.C. will be a potential problem and we have over sixty thousand of them!"

"Surely you can control that Art?" Alexander challenged.

"We should have more control, but not all the interfaces are known, some are necessary...anyway it may be too late even as we speak!" Art sounded conciliatory; he did not know the extent of this problem and decided to cut the explanation short.

"Thirdly, in a project this large errors are inevitable, the problem is we will not know the extent of this until it is too late." He hesitated for a few seconds the continued. "My worry on this is that some of the companies we used to correct the problem may well be out of business as of now. Who will stick around for this kind of liability?" The words sounded ominous. "Let us assess this as a five percent probability," he guessed again for completeness, then added. "You should be aware that we are already experiencing problems with our networks in Asia, which our experts are trying to resolve."

"Do you think you are typical of all industry?" The President asked sternly.

"Bearing in mind that the insurance industry has been working on this problem the longest, it would be prudent to expect that we are the best case Mr. President!" he said firmly.

"Hell Art, you're telling me nothing...and you're the best case!" the President rattled the group. The pleasant mood suddenly turned sour. "What can I expect, when can I expect it and what can I do about it?" His questions were sharp, rapid, and designed to provoke.

"I can't answer the first two questions but our early thoughts are, that if we had to do it again, we would switch everything off at midnight December 31 and slowly bring back up at 12.01 local time at every location," Art added. "Only adding compliant locations to our network, but that is in hindsight now!" The telephone fell silent. The confrontation was over.

The President looked troubled. Even though he understood the immensity of the problem, he did not want his inner fears confirmed. "Why have we not heard more from other Governments pressed the President?"

"Several reasons come to mind," volunteered Raymond, who instantly regretted the interruption as the President's eyes focussed on him.

He rose unsteadily feeling self-conscious now "Firstly January 1, 2000 is both a Saturday and a holiday and there just may not be experienced personnel around to diagnose any of the problems. Raymond paused and swallowed hard. "Secondly, embarrassment …even disbelief, or just plain incompetence in understanding the business ramifications. Thirdly, "Fear" ... he groped for the right words. " Fear of legal liability from anyone who cares to claim damages, such as customers, shareholders, suppliers, perhaps even employees."

The last comment prompted an anguished question from the President. "Are any government agencies in this mess also?" he gasped fearing the worst.

The Vice President felt obliged to contribute, "It would appear that there will be some crises to address, by just extrapolating Arts previous point, about the errors, which will inevitably occur. I think the IRS is apprehensive, as is the Social Security Department, who will be in the main line of fire, if checks cannot be produced. We cut thirty two billion dollars, per week, in Social Security and payroll checks. Even a short delay will cause shock waves throughout the economy. The Department of Transport was always a laggard and could not complete conversion of its six hundred and thirty critical systems, disruption will almost certainly occur!"

"Unbelievable!" exclaimed Alexander, unable to hide his frustration. "What about the military?" The President snapped, looking hard at the Vice President.

Scott flushed then began. "As you know the Department of Defense was always behind schedule and we will not know the full effects until problems happen. Also the error factor is totally unknown!" He said lamely.

"Will this affect our ability to respond to any threat?" the President pursued the issue, his tone was harsh. His penetrating eyes now boring through Alex Scott, who always felt the brunt of Alexander's frustration.

"If disruption does occur there will be contingency plans put into action by every service!" Scott replied, with more authority.

Everyone was now subconsciously holding their breath as the magnitude of the crises began to dawn on them. The tension made the room seem claustrophobic, only one man capable of breaking the mood. No one made eye contact for a full minute as The President paced the room looking slowly at the group. To Raymond he looked somehow smaller than before, as if this new knowledge had burdened him physically.

"Well Gentlemen!" The spell was broken as the Alexander began, "comments and suggestions, please?" This was more a command than a request.

Scott jumped in again, "We should contact the UN immediately," he blurted out and then added, "And get the Joint Chiefs of Staff together."

Woodward, up until now an observer added. "All Government Agencies should be contacted for status reports! I know they have published quarterly reports but today's status is required."

The conference phone squawked as Prezzano volunteered.

"A joint team of CIA and Global should tackle the funds and armaments issue! Sir."

Alexander's eyes flared, "Ah yes," he began "how real is the terrorist threat?" He questioned.

Sloan answered, "It is too early to say for certain, but that we think there is enough circumstantial evidence to warrant further investigation!"

The President drew a deep breath, and exhaled slowly, he seemed temporarily satisfied with the responses and slowly regained his composure. The redness was draining from his face and his demeanor was softening; however, his lips were pressed thin and bloodless. He surveyed the room then asked pointedly for Scott to take responsibility for getting the Joint Chiefs of Staff together and the Directors of all the main government Agencies. He asked John Sloan and Art Gregory to develop a plan for Global's problem. "You can use the White House facilities and count on Military support if require...Let's meet in one hour!" he fired, as he made his way to the door. Hesitating briefly he asked Alex Scott to join him and they both quietly left the room.

In the vacuum left by the President and Vice President's departure John Sloan's voice pierced the deadly silence. "Gentlemen, perhaps we should divide into two groups," he suggested, "one involving the general issue of the millennium bug and one involving the robbery and armaments problem."

They all agreed.

"Let's have Raymond, Sally, Al, Mike and Art's team get together. Hank and myself will help Alex Scott pull together the Government Departments."

John took note of everyone's telephone numbers and signed off. He turned to those in the oval office and suggested that they forage for food, quarters and support.

"The next few hours are going to be hell" he grated. The words were left hanging in the room as he and Hank left.

ACTION

CHAPTER 15

The anticlimactic feeling after the meeting verged on depressing, and there was a desperate silence in the oval office. All the energy seemed to have left the room with the President. For Raymond this never-ending day was draining his very existence. He needed to sleep, or at least, have some private time to think. Inertia had overcome the small group who were now reluctant to leave the comfort and safety of the Oval Office, which, strangely gave them a sense of security against the outside world.

Not one of them had experienced the inner workings of the White House before, so they were all in uncharted waters. The fear of breaking protocol became an inhibitor to progress, although no one would admit it. Raymond for one was grateful for the brief respite, and sat, lost in his own thoughts, thankful that at least he had Sally by his side.

The entrance of a very officious looking aide broke the somber mood. Raymond groaned under his breath as he dragged himself to his feet in expectation of the group's redeployment to less auspicious surroundings.

"If you would follow me Gentlemen?" The aide commenced. "I'll show you to one of our conference rooms," and he guided the group from the room.

They followed the Aide, in silence, through what seemed like a labyrinth of corridors, to a well lit and tastefully decorated room, capable of holding about twenty people. Standing in the center of the room was a large oval rosewood conference table, to the side were matching servers and a small china cabinet. There were four white telephones sitting on side tables at each corner of the room. Note pads and pens with the White House insignia were prominently on display. The room looked comfortable, almost luxurious but the group immediately sensed it was used for serious work.

The Aide was dressed in a formal military uniform and addressed the group as if they were all generals. "Refreshments are on their way, the restrooms were two doors down on the right, and the telephones were secure!" He said respectfully.

The small group was impressed by his efficiency and nodded in acknowledgement that things were satisfactory.

The young man backed out of the room asking "If anything else is required please call extension 587 and ask for David!"

The bathroom was everyone's immediate priority for R. & R. Repair and Reinvigoration and when they returned to the conference room one of the servers held sodas coffee, sandwiches, cookies, crockery and silverware.

Tension had made everyone so thirsty, that drinks became their first priority. The sandwiches and cookies were only picked over; somehow they all had lost their appetites.

Sipping his third cup of coffee, Al Pagano suggested, "We better touch base with Dave Prezzano, Arthur Gregory and Joe Kielak at Global." He fumbled with the note that held the telephone numbers and dialed the first number.

"Hello!" Prezzano was waiting for the call and answered immediately. "Any further developments?" He asked.

"No, not yet, I'm about to call Global, please hold the line." He dialed Kielak "Hello Joe, we are ready this end, is Art with you?"

"No he asked us to begin without him, he'll catch up with us!"

Pagano began "Perhaps I should summarize the facts again then we can devise a response!"

"Good idea Al, go ahead!" Sloan said flatly.

"One, large fund transfers seem to terminate in Lahaina on the island of Maui. Two, A ship carrying arms appears to be heading for Honolulu, presumably for some kind of rendezvous, and three, at least some of Global's employees are involved and may be in Hawaii"

Everyone concurred with the summation.

Al then thew a question to Dave Prezzano "What would be the expected sequences of occurrences in such a transaction?"

Dave had studied and experienced the practices of terrorists for thirteen years. He preempted his answer. "These people get more creative every year, however, the main elements of the transaction would be involve the following;

- Inspection of the arms by the buyers to verify the equipment was per the contract.
- Agreed delivery time, place, etc.,
- Transfer of money or other assets,
- Disappearance by all."

Al interrupted, "Under our scenario, where would this transaction most likely to take place?" he pressed.

"Normally, I would say it could be anywhere in the Hawaiian

Islands Kauai being my first guess. But with this millennium bug issue and the uncertainty of funds getting to the right place at the right time, my thoughts are that it must be a cash transaction. It's an awful lot of cash however. Possibilities include Honolulu, but I doubt whether the Kingfisher will venture so close to our coastguard!" He paused. "If it is Maui? i.e. the note is not a red herring, and then two locations are possible; Kahului and Lahaina! But, again I'm not sure they could handle the cash! There must be another wrinkle," he added. "I would chose Kahului for a quick escape as it has an airport. Lahaina is a port so escape could be by a high powered boat!"

The others listened intently and concluded that these deductions were all reasonable.

Dave continued, "For a cash transaction to occur, people capable of authorizing such large transactions would have to be present at the bank to withdraw the money!"

"So we start with the bank!" Raymond surmised.

"Yes, that would be my guess!"

"What alternatives do we have?" Pagano asked.

"Very little," Prezzano replied, "I think it is a long shot but we should concentrate our efforts on Maui, Lahaina in particular, if that is where the bank is!"

"What resources would be required?" Kielak asked.

"We will need the coast guard, cooperation of local police, and any CIA operatives in the area, would be helpful," Prezzano's voice was flat. "Anyone who can identify Global's employees would be a huge plus," he added. "We could also request our National Surveillance Agency to try and locate the ship. Their satellites can identify the date on a quarter from over 100 miles up. Only problem is it will take time for them to realign their orbit if they have to, I'm not hopeful on that one!"

The resources available impressed Raymond but doubted that they could be marshaled in time. "Time was something in short supply right now," he broke in, then added, "We should also cover the other countries potentially involved, for instance it looks as if a crime has already been committed in New Zealand and Australia. If we can get our hands on the people there, it may help us here."

"Good idea!" Prezzano volunteered.

Kielak entered the conversation again, "Looks like you guys have everything covered, the only thing we can do is monitor our network for cash transfers and for clues and get you photographs of our thief, if possible."

Sally contributed "I think I can identify the person responsible for the transfer of cash in Lahaina. I think his name is John McKenzie." She turned to Raymond and said, "You know him also Raymond."

Raymond looked at her in astonishment "The Boston Radio license." He muttered under his breath.

"Getting anyone to Lahaina in time would be impossible!" Pagano interrupted.

"A Phantom IV will do the trick," Prezzano said, matter of fact, the metallic voice sounded slightly arrogant.

"Looks as if we have the skeleton of a plan," Pagano smiled with satisfaction.

The group were in agreement, however they were not yet convinced that it could be described as anywhere near a plan. They had ten minutes before they would meet again with the President.

Al Pagano agreed to try to brief John Sloan if he could find him, and left the others in the conference room. He passed a conference room two doors down on the same side as theirs.

Pagano caught Sloan's eye who was sitting facing the open door. Sloan waved Pagano in. This meeting was less acrimonious than theirs had been, Pagano could feel the atmosphere was thick with politics, positioning and shear resentment at being summoned to the White House on New Years Eve, either physically or by telephone. There had been accusations about misinformation, ignorance and overzealousness regarding the whole subject, but underlying all the accusations, there was a distinct smell of embarrassment and fear by the accusers.

Alex Scott sat in silent rage; his thin bloodless lips made him appear uncharacteristically dangerous. Usually seen as a moderate man, the people around the table were becoming disturbed by his demeanor. The bluster of several people talking at the same time slowly dissipated, until there was complete silence. Scott stood up; "Gentlemen I must emphasize that this is a real issue and problems are even now being experienced elsewhere in the world, although we have received no official notice as yet!"

An aide approached him and passed an official looking document, he scanned it then addressed the group.

"I have just received a report from the National Surveillance Agency that our Geosats, which incidentally are still operating for now, have picked up some unusual activity."

Scott paused, placing his reading glasses on, which gave him an owlish look, he held the report away from him and read.

"There appears to be an oil rig ablaze in the Indian Ocean just off Burma's coastline. About an acre of sea is on fire! In the Middle East there is activity in the oil fields, which support the theory of a disruption in oil flow from most of the fields. Coincidentally there is a build up of troops on the Iraqi border with Kuwait; we are not sure if these two items are related or how to interpret either at the moment." He paused to let the gravity of his words sink in.

"In Russia there seems to be a migration in progress away from the area surrounding the Tomsk Nuclear Power Station." He took a sip of water before adding, "I hope this is not another Chernobyl!"

The secretary for energy interrupted, "Is this data verified?"

Scott looked up; "Communication is so poor we cannot verify these events through normal channels. Our current policy is to cautiously believe these reports!" The room was silent, some shaking their heads in disbelief.

"You should also aware that several of our banks have informed us that 'Joe Public' has been withdrawing cash from their accounts fearful of losing it. I hope our system is robust to stand this!"

"We should be alright Sir!" a deputy director from Treasury ventured the answer nervously.

Scott smiled weakly and continued, "We should take these reports as a warning and be even more prepared then we might have been. There will be no winners in this game because if we have no problems it is only what the general public expects. I urge you to be objective and realistic in your assessment of the situation and again verify priorities and contingency plans so that I can inform the President." He used silence to effectively emphasize that he was deadly serious. Scott began moving towards the door "I have to leave to meet with the President again, when I come back I would like to have a list of potential problems, prioritized with suggestions about contingency plans." He looked over to John Sloan and Hank Woodward who made a move to join him and they left the room trailed by Pagano.

"How did your meeting go?" Sloan asked Pagano grimly, as they walked toward the Oval Office.

"Quite well" enthused Pagano. "In fact we have a skeleton plan to review with you, but as you know time is at a premium."

"Yes indeed!" responded Sloan. But he was lost in his own thoughts about the last meeting; it was times like these when he wished he had never left his own business.

By the time the four of them entered the oval office the President had gleaned a good deal of the plan from Raymond, Sally and Carey and was looking more than a little pleased. Raymond was in mid sentence when the Vice President and the others entered, and after a brief interruption he was allowed to continue.

"The teleconference attendees left it with us to inform you, however they all agree with the plan. But I'll let Mr. Pagano give you the final details," Raymond gestured for his boss to take the floor.

Pagano virtually glowed in his brief period in the spot light on what could, arguably be, the world's greatest stage. Pagano talked slow and deliberately to savor his moment, having difficulty hiding the slight smile that appeared on his face. He highlighted the resources that would be needed. "We – we would like to use the Geosats to track the whereabouts of the Kingfisher," he stuttered. " Mobilization of the coast guard in Honolulu, to search for the Kingfisher, would also be desirable" he looked solemnly at the stern faces. "The police chief in Lahaina should be informed and assistance sent to him in the form of Sally and Raymond." He hesitated now, as the request for two Phantom IV's to transport them to Hawaii seemed somewhat presumptuous, his brow became furrowed with apprehension. "We require to two air force jets to fly Raymond and Sally to Maui as soon as possible!" his face was flushed now. "Finally, Australian and New Zealand intelligence agencies should be given full details of what we know and perhaps, local assistance given to help apprehend the criminals downunder!" Pagano finished, smiling slightly he looked around the room at his silent audience. He took a deep breath and his chest swelled visibly when he noticed an approving look on Alexander's face.

The plan was easy to understand so it was not difficult for the President to buy into it. Alexander stood up; still smiling but it looked forced. It was hard to determine his genuine feelings. "Gentlemen ... Thank you for your thoughts and efforts, simplicity is the best route," he continued with surprising firmness. "Arrangements will be made for full cooperation to be given by the necessary services, he paused. "It is a go!" Thank you again for your vigilance on this important issue, and God Bless America, I think we will need his help."

He moved over to his desk and picked up the phone and rattled a series of orders into the speaker, seconds later his assistant appeared and invited Raymond and Sally to follow her. They both stood up; shook hands with everyone then trailed the young woman as she left the room. A series of good byes and good luck reverberated around the room and followed them into the hallway.

An air force helicopter slowly landed on the White House lawn, as Raymond and Sally left the comfort of the White House. They haunched over, like most people who approach a helicopter and moved slowly towards the aircraft. A young lieutenant jumped down, saluted them, and then helped them inside. After securing the couples' seat-belts he signaled to the pilot who immediately took off and headed in the direction of Langley Air Force Base, where two Phantom IV's were preparing to fly them to Hawaii at over twice the speed of sound.

Pagano and Carey were whisked off by car to CIA headquarters where they tried to inform the authorities on Maui and police and Intelligence Agencies in Australia, Hong Kong, New Zealand, Switzerland and London.

The President, Vice President and the two Directors' sat quietly reflecting somberly on the morning's meetings, as the others left the Oval office. No one spoke, but their thoughts held little hope for success, the task was more than likely to fail due, mainly, to the lack of time. That lack of time and problems with communication prevented the mobilization of experienced operatives who would be fully trained, briefed and prepared for every eventuality. A crisis team normally would have all the latest information, technology, contacts and back up available to ensure a reasonable chance of success.

In contrast the hasty deployment of two inexperienced people looking for a vaguely familiar face in a strange city dealing with unknown contacts and unreliable communications, would stand no chance at all. They were all thinking how impossible it was, but it was the best that could be done under the circumstances. Alexander's thoughts had a political bias; "At least the Government could not be accused of inaction should these details ever come to light. Indeed political kudos should result just with the dissemination of the information gathered by the CIA, even if the resultant action failed." He was also worried about the terrorist activity on US soil disturbing thoughts resonated in his mind. The apprehension and containment of terrorist and illegal weapons could eventually prove to be an embarrassment. There was always the possibility of retaliation and the situation would require some fine juggling on the stage of the world's politics to appease the opposing interests of the countries involved. Alexander made a mental note to redirect some of the promised resources allocated to the project just in case someone got lucky.

"What's next on the Agenda Alex?" the President demanded, breaking the oppressive mood.

"Well Sir, this millennium bug problem has generated a great deal of indignity with the staff. As you know, all the departments had allocated considerable time and resources so they would be prepared for this issue. They acknowledge that errors will occur but have contingency plans and will respond to the hiccups as they occur!"

"How did they respond to the incidents overseas?" The President asked.

"They firmly believe that the U.S.A. leads the way in preparedness!" Scott responded.

Alexander's eyes narrowed "If that's the case what are our responsibilities in helping the rest of the world cope with any major problems?" The President pressed, not believing the previous answer.

"That has not yet been considered by us, in fact when we left the meeting they were charged with reviewing and prioritizing possible problems here in the U.S.A." Scott paused. "If they do this jointly it may be a model we can share with the UN," he offered.

"Good, Good," murmured the President." Shall we see what they have for us?"

All four stood up together. The President led the way out to meet "Le dissidents en masses."

The mood in the conference room was much more productive than when Al Scott had left. The in fighting and ass covering rhetoric had stopped and there seemed to be an atmosphere of cooperation, or so Scott thought. His only apprehension was how they would react in the presence of their leader. "Would this cooperative mood prevail would showmanship take its place?"

"Gentlemen," the President greeted them cordially. "Thank you for coming to the White House on such short notice, I hope you are being treated well?" The false smile reappeared. "I think you appreciate the subject's importance and I know you all have this matter under control, at least as much as reasonably possible." He scanned the audience slowly for any reaction. "Our objectives are perhaps two fold. One to review our status here in the U.S.A. and perhaps to identify some gaps, and two, to see if we can offer the world any assistance. Any Questions?" Alexander sounded curt.

General Richard A. Lee of the army was the first to direct a question to his Chief of Staff. "Sir, we understand the general nature of your concern, but could you clarify whether it involves each departments' support for its own efforts, or, how the Government services could support business at large?" he said brusquely.

Like all generals, Lee was a career soldier used to hearing explanations rather than giving them. His directness was often mistaken for rudeness and impatience, but all present were used to his demeanor and rarely took exception. Lee was a short man with steely gray hair, more like steel wool. His gray blue eyes were dispassionate and his round face and ruddy complexion gave the false impression that he was a jovial person. His thin lips rarely smiled and hid a perfect set of pearly white teeth. Lee sat motionless waiting for a response.

The President began his answer. "I've heard this Y2K project described as the world's largest, save perhaps World War II. The money and people involved are comparable, so like World War II we will have many surprises to contend with, both within our control and also extraneous to our control. The more we are prepared the fewer the surprises will be."

Lee unconsciously showed his frustration, he could never understand politicians. "You ask a simple direct question requiring a simple direct answer and you get another vote catching speech. " If there's not a war to win let's create one,'' he thought, "to deflect the public's attention from the broken election promises."

The audience began to clear their throats and shuffled impatiently, they wanted this meeting over as soon as possible. No more questions were asked, and resentment re-entered the room

Al Scott jumped in and asked what issues had been identified.

Gary Powell Director of Trade and Industry stood up and waved a piece of paper, he began "Everyone had identified potentially critical issues, but possible solutions had not been discussed as yet." He read from the list mechanically.

"One - In the coldest regions, concern would be over any loss of power generation and transfer for any length of time. Two - Nuclear reactors subjected to involuntary close downs may present serious problems. Three - Chemical and Petroleum plants controlled by systems may become extremely hazardous. Four - Dam malfunctions causing flooding would be serious in some locations. Loss of drinking water would be particularly serious, this could also occur if pumping stations malfunction. Five - Satellite outages could be dangerous, as would the loss of air traffic control systems. Six - Civil unrest could occur due to breakdown in cash distribution, gas distribution, power distribution, etc. Seven - Some facilities are more vulnerable than others to disruptions of services, hospitals, prisons, and airports, each have auxiliary equipment, but this may not kick in. Eight - of course any compromise situation to military capability could be dangerous," he paused then added, "But this is unlikely!"

"Eight important areas!" Alexander commented, "Any other issues?"

"We felt that food distribution did not pose a lasting threat unless there was significant hoarding nor would individual transportation problems due to inoperative traffic signals, however, emergency services would be under great strain. We should probably warn such organizations as The Red Cross and The Salvation Army!" Powell paused again and speculated. "Export and Imports could slow down as could the distribution of spare parts for repairs but this would not be a long-term issue. Chaos could result in the lost or erroneous reimbursement programs, from Government departments!" He took a sip of water. "The previous items were considered important but not life threatening."

"Internet trade may collapse temporarily." This was more speculation than fact but no one was prepared to argue.

"Processing of people through immigration and security checks at ports of entry could be flash points. The recent run on the banks appears to be irrational due to the fact that most deposits are insured by the FDIC but we should advertise this fact soon!" He nodded slightly indicating he had finished and sat down.

"I think this covered everything," Powell concluded.

"A very thorough synopsis" The President complimented "It would be catastrophic to experience several of the failures simultaneously," his mind was racing now. "The problem seems to be the randomness with which things could fail or just the uncertainty."

Powell continued: "The randomness is due in large part to the multitude of systems and control devices and how they interact. A microprocessor in a machine may not fail in itself, but may pass invalid dates to the control system, which could react differently in a different program environment. The uncertainty comes about by the lack of knowledge of what is out there. A control system could have been reprogrammed without adequate documentation, a microchip replaced without knowledge. There's not much in the way of accurate records when you really get down to it. It's scary how technologically dependent we have become without knowing its consequences." Powell thought aloud.

The President posed a rhetorical question to no one in particular. "Suppose we are 99% compliant, What does that other 1% represent and will be 1% interact with the 99% in a way to make some greater proportion non-compliant?"

The meeting was getting bogged down in the enormity of the issue. This was a once in a lifetime problem, there was no past experience to lean on, and as such Y2K defied total comprehension. There was a desperate silence now as individual comprehension. There was a desperate silence now as individual minds grappled with insoluble problems. Academia would have welcomed such lofty problems and thoughts but frustration was the emotion that invaded this meeting, now.

Powell again, "What you have here is a weakest link issue. You can have individually compliant systems vulnerable at their weakest link. What may happen is multiple overlapping failures, not large individual events, a series of Y2K storms if you like to describe it! Some will be innocuous and some will be disastrous, however, all will happen in the same time frame." Powell fell silent momentarily. "I think an analogy could be that anyone can replace two or three light bulbs in a house, if they break, even going to the store and buying them, - no big deal; but if all the light bulbs in town went out – different problem! Supply shortage, prioritization issues, loss of control, etc., etc.,"

This scenario did nothing to improve the mood pervading the room.

John Sloan broke the tension drawing on his past business acumen and drive to action. "Perhaps the only thing we can consider is to assemble a rapid response team to advise local crises teams. If we do this in the U.S.A. it could form the axle of a global effort. That is, providing communications are reliable."

The words hung heavy in the charged atmosphere. Slowly nods of agreement were reluctantly given under the pressure of Alexander's stare.

"Who would define the parameters and assemble such a team?" Alexander requested.

"I think initially, it should be largely populated by the forces, however, companies like IBM, Microsoft, Etc. could be asked to volunteer technical resources in due course!" Sloan proposed. "The National Guard should also be put on alert, as a contingency, and the armed forces would stand by to help in any way feasible!"

"Yes, I agree! Can I ask you to lead this effort?" He turned to his Vice President.

"Of course Sir," Alex Scott replied softly.

General Lee stood up, "Sir," He looked around his peers, "We did not address the issue of troop build up on the Kuwait border! Is it conceivable that they plan an attack while we deal with the other problems?"

Alexander looked grave, "It is conceivable," he paused, "If they think we will be incapacitated they may strike....but we have no way to confirm their intentions. We need to meet separately on this issue."

The next step was for the President to arrange a meeting with the Secretary of the United Nations to exchange ideas.

CHAPTER 16

The small Russian made Jeep was approaching Rumalia in Southern Iraq about one hundred miles north of the Kuwait border. General Hassan of the vaunted Republican Guard was in the passenger seat squinting hard to see the air force base, which was his destination. Driving him was Major Kizam, a long time friend who stared steadfastly at the dark road in front of him. The jeep headlights barely helped. He glanced at the General. "Is this an exercise or the real thing?" The General stared ahead, not turning his eyes from the road;

"It all depends on the status of their technological weapons!" came the vague reply.

The Major frowned waiting for an explanation. He looked back at the other two jeeps doggedly following them in the V like formation to avoid the fine sand particles as they formed blinding dust clouds.

The General continued.... "Due to their capitalistic stupidity years ago, it seems that America and Europe have made a bad mistake with their computer systems. At midnight tonight, our technical people tell us that their so called smart weapons may not work," he said evenly, pausing to find the right words. "Something to do with the year change to two thousand, which computers read as nineteen hundred." The General shook his head slowly.

Major Kizam drove on, disbelief written all over his face, he glanced at Hassan. "Do you really believe this General?" He decelerated and swerved to miss a rock, then pressed his foot down again, Kizam continued. "It seems unbelievable, too far fetched." He paused. "Our people must be reading too much western fiction."

Both were peering out, looking for landmarks as they plunged across the desert in the dead of night. The General sat relaxed and incredibly composed as the jeep bounced over the poor excuse for a road.

"It's our job to find out," he said eventually is a low purposeful voice

"Even now they might be having difficulties with their spy satellites." He looked skyward as if he could see the orbiting devices, then glanced at his Seiko watch, eleven-twenty, "We're fifteen minutes over our deadline" a tinge of impatience crept into his voice.

The major put his foot down and accelerated causing particles of sand to burst in his wake. He kept his foot to the floor and turned on the narrow beamed fog light, to help the misnamed headlights. They both peered into a cloudless sky searching for the perimeter lights of the airfield without result. Above them they heard the distant drone of an aircraft. The general picked up his night light binoculars and scanned the horizon.

"There it is," he said, pointing to the southeast. The airfield rose out of the shapeless and desolate sands. "We'll be there in fifteen minutes," he estimated.

The sound of the aircraft grew louder; it was circling at a very low altitude unconcerned about detection or combat possibilities. The jeep approached a security outpost and slowed, lights blazed around the area and the general looked over the scene, without emotion. No attempt had been taken to hide the twenty Mirage Fighters, which had flown down from Baghdad only hours before. Some of the ground crews were frantically working on three of them, their pilots standing by anxiously, at the end of the airfield. There was a small fleet of lightly armed helicopters whose sole mission was to transport ground troops to specific targets, when and if the orders were given.

The guard saluted as the three jeeps passed through security; smiling to himself as he noted that the officers were all caked in a layer of fine gray brownish dust, giving them a ghost like appearance.

General Hassan instructed Major Kizam to make straight for the officers' quarters where he was expected. "We'll inspect the base later," he added.

Kizam turned the wheel briskly and headed for a single story building about two hundred meters away, the other jeeps followed automatically. Kizam and Hassan jumped out and dusted themselves down as a figure approached them.

"Welcome General!" Major Aziz stood at attention. "This way please," he ushered Hassan and Kizam into a small room occupied by half a dozen officers, who stood to attention, anticipation written all over their faces. The officers saluted, silence befell the room.

"At ease gentlemen!" Hassan smiled. "You must be wondering why we have been mobilized, especially now!"

The men nodded and murmured uneasily.

He chose to stand with his hands on his hips, legs about two feet apart. "We have received word that, at midnight, our enemy's technological weapons will become ineffective, some computer glitch" he smiled wryly. "This problem has been known for some time and efforts have been made to correct it," he paused, "but our experts think that the Allies underestimated the problem and ran out of time!" He looked directly at each face trying to read their reaction. "Our job is to test whether their weapons are, in fact, useless."

The officers stared at each other afraid to speak.

"We will do this by engaging in exercises near the Kuwait border, this should prompt a quick retaliation. If there is none then we will prepare to invade Kuwait again and take our revenge! Any questions?" He asked brusquely.

His audience could not believe their ears and shuffled nervously.

"How will we know that their weapons are useless?" Captain Mohamed asked in a raspy voice, his eyes danced sharply around the room in nervous fashion.

"If they hesitate to warn us off, this will show weakness, their fighters should respond within hours if they are effective. Our planes will remain here unless we request them so any aircraft flying will be the enemy's!" He paused. "This is an ideal time for us, we must be courageous in our fight against Western oppression," the General was relying on their obedience.

"Are we ready for such an operation General?" Major Aziz queried nervously.

"As you know we have been preparing for this for months, bringing troops and equipment down here for exercises, returning with dummies. As far as we know the allies do not know our ground force strength here so we will have an element of surprise." He walked over to a map hanging on the wall and outlined the plan, with a wooden pointer. "At 0400 hours, two platoons will move into the desert, one will move Northwest, and the other Northeast for about two hours. Both will then turn due South, which will bring them close to the Kuwait border around 0800 hours. The timing is designed to coincide with midnight, Washington time. If our technical people are correct there will be serious disruption in communication systems, around the world during this period and chaos will result."

His audience shuffled uncomfortably, the noise of chairs scraping the floor, filled the room. Some Officers coughed nervously; their throats dry with fear.

"Will our systems not be affected also?" Captain Mohamed asked hesitantly.

"No, our VHF radio's, anything which depends on satellites or normal channels may be, but our local equipment should be alright. We will test our systems after midnight local time!" He automatically glanced at his watch. "In fact we can commence now!" The digital watch indicated 00.40. "We have had our Muslim cousins from India, who have specialized in this problem, check our equipment and they have said we should not experience any issues."

The group looked more optimistic now, the mood in the room changed as courage and hope replaced nervousness.

"Now Gentlemen, shall we inspect the troops?" Hassan said firmly indicating that the briefing was over. He nodded to Major Kizam who handed out specific written orders to each officer, the room fell silent as they read their own particular part in this tragic play. No more questions were asked and they were dismissed with the customary salute.

Thirty minutes later Hassan inspected the assault troops and equipment. "I compliment you on your preparedness, Major Aziz, good work, may you be triumphant over our enemies tonight!" He saluted stiffly.

At 0400 hours the tanks left the southern part of the airfield, amidst coughing carburetors and the steady roar of diesel

Engines and turning north, they disappeared into a featureless landscape and unknown destiny.

"We will see how ready the Allies really are!" Hassan said quietly.

CHAPTER 17

It had been 30 minutes since Raymond and Sally had left Langley Airforce Base and both were waiting for their stomachs to catch up with them. They were traveling due West at Mach II, about sixteen hundred miles per hour, in two state of the art fighter planes. The Phantom IV was a newly commissioned two-seater attack plane designed to give rapid support to ground and naval combat units. It was capable of traveling at well over Mach II on a sustained basis, as were the pilots, however, the two civilian passengers were not.

The Phantom was a derivative of the SR-71 "*The Blackbird*" which was developed in the early 1990's by Lockheed. It was powered by two Pratt & Whitney J58 engines each producing 32500 lbs. of thrust, giving the plane a maximum speed of two thousand, two hundred miles per hour at altitudes in excess of eighty five thousand feet, just less than seventeen miles. They had been used to study deep space objects in wavelengths that are blocked from ground based equipment. The SR71 utilized revolutionary equipment such as laser light to measure airspeed and altitude. These particular "*Phantoms*" used a unique aerodynamic false bottom to significantly reduce the peak of the sonic boom. This allowed the aircraft to observe ground-based objects as well as celestial images. Basically a two-seater jet, this versatility to monitor both downward and upward objects required that the fuselage be modified in order to take a third person. This modification altered the plane's performance somewhat, but not significantly enough to comfort Raymond or Sally. They were both fighting to keep the rising sickness at bay after experiencing the G4 pressure of the aircraft's rapid climbing rate. Their excitement about flying the most advanced plane in the world was short lived and their only thoughts now were of being back on the terra firma.

When they left the White House the helicopter whisked them to Langley, where they were shown to rooms to change into jump suits. They also took advantage of the showering facilities, something Raymond was particularly thankful for. Due to the time constraints, they declined food and drink, which would prove to be a wise choice, and while waiting for the aircraft's routine flight check both chose to make telephone calls.

Raymond caught up with Al Pagano at his office phone. "Our contact in Sydney has seen Kelly, he's accompanied by an unknown woman," he blurted out. The Australian Security Agency should contact him!"

Pagano acknowledged the information. "What's his address?" he asked

"I'll get back to you on that!' Raymond cursed at himself for not being prepared He immediately tried to phone Jon but could not get through. He asked the duty officer if he could use a HF radio and was shown to a communications center, a young signalman reached Jon.

"Hey, what's with you?" Raymond queried

"I'm o.k." Jon replied, somewhat surprised to hear Raymond's voice.

"I'm on my way to Hawaii," Raymond blurted out a smile crossed his face. "It's a tough life but someone's got to do it!"

"Some people have all the luck," an unenthusiastic reply made it from Australia.

"There are two things I need. "What is your address? So that I can inform my boss, and keep a lookout for any mention of a ship called the Kingfisher." Raymond was rushing now.

Jon was breathless at the speed of events and was exhilarated at his involvement in the International Espionage. The two men exchanged contact information. Raymond then left Jon's address in Al Pagano's voice mail.

Pagano had already deployed the coast guard but could not get access to the satellites of the National Surveillance Agency. He was on he phone with the Chief of Police in Maui, when Raymond had called him back and noticed that he had voice mail. Mike Carey was tracking down their nearest agent skilled in counter-terrorism activity to assist the team, but had no information for them yet. All had gone remarkably smoothly up until now. Their next tasks were to contact the Asian and European authorities.

The Phantoms were now approaching Wailuku, the Capital of Maui, and the descent proved to be equally uncomfortable as the ascent. As there were no military bases on Maui special clearance was obtained for the jets to land at the Civilian airfield, the reason given was a technical emergency.

The final approach of the *Phantoms* became much more tolerable to Sally who looked out of the cockpit at the magnificent azure blue sea, white velvet sand and lush green foliage below her. This was her first time in Maui and she marveled at its beauty. The cinder cone of the ten thousand-foot Volcano dominated the landscape and Sally had a bird's eye view of this natural wonder. Raymond missed all this majesty lost in his own thoughts on what was to be done. He was preoccupied with the increasingly formidable task in front of him.

The two jets approached the sleepy airport together, one slightly behind and to the port side of the other plane. The noise over the island was deafening but only the locals noticed this, as unusual. Visiting tourists were oblivious to the strange unfolding of events taking place. The lead jet lowered its landing gear, flared out and hit the tarmac hard, reversing thrusts immediately, brakes screamed and smoked as the jet struggled to land on the short runway. The pilot taxied to some corrugated iron buildings, used for storage, near the end of the runway and turned off the powerful engines returning the small island to its former peacefulness. The second jet repeated the exercise. Raymond deplaned and rushed over to help Sally, both were pleased to be on tarmac again and were bending and stretching to chase away the muscle cramping.

A police car drove out from the terminal followed by a small van. The local chief of Police Jacob Smith jumped out of the front passenger seat and strode towards them.

"Welcome to Maui," he beamed. "I'm Jacob Smith!" He held out his hand "Quite an entrance, if I may say so!" he looked at the strange aircraft.

"We're just glad to get here." Raymond's face showed his relief; he offered Jacob his hand, somewhat unsteadily. "This is Sally Damen!"

Jacob took her hand and kissed it, European style. Sally flushed unexpectedly.

Raymond glanced at his watch, "Um! … Six p.m., Washington time," he thought. He turned to Jacob, "What time is it?"

"Twelve noon," Jacob replied.

Raymond looked pleased, "We've gained an hour, the wonders of time travel!" he joked.

" This way please" Jacob turned and led them to a waiting police van.

"Here are some clothes for you to make you less conspicuous," he looked at their jump suits and smiled. "Unfortunately you will have to change in the van."

They both climbed into the van and helped each other dress in bright island shirts and khakis.

During this time the Phantoms were refueled under the supervision of the pilots, ready for their short trip to Honolulu which would, as ordered, commence as soon as possible.

Raymond and Sally emerged from the van, still dressing and waved enthusiastically to the pilots. Jacob directed them to an unmarked police Jeep Cherokee; they jumped into the rear seat as it moved off in the direction of Lahaina. The police van went in the opposite direction.

The journey took forty-two minutes during which Jacob related his understanding of the situation as discussed with Al Pagano.

Jacob Smith was a very likable man who had lived all his life on the island. His ancestors had mixed blood, so he was light skinned. His black curly hair was cut military short, and he had big mischievous looking brown eyes, but his most endearing feature was a large toothy grin, which he used with great effect.

"It is my understanding," Jacob addressed Raymond, "that we are looking for a white person called John McKenzie, who must be using an alias, as we have no records of his arrival. Also we are looking for a cargo ship called *Kingfisher* which may dock in our vicinity," his island accent gave a melodic ring to his voice.

"Correct on both counts!" Raymond confirmed.

"To identify this man will be difficult because the Island is full of holiday makers for the New Year festivities. Every hotel room is taken. In fact we can only offer you rooms at me and my deputy's house, or at the jailhouse," he grinned mischievously. 'And I expect the jail to be full tonight."

Raymond acknowledged the kindness of his offer, "I suspect the jail house will do as we will have to watch the International Island Bank most of the time, at least until the money leaves." Jacob was still grinning but hoped that this duty would be over soon so he could enjoy the parties he was invited to. Serious crime was not high on his agenda tonight.

Lahaina appeared through the windshield, it had a very colorful town center, with a multitude of brightly colored buildings lining the main street. Traffic was not very heavy; a few brightly colored Chevy and Ford taxis made their way slowly to and from the hotels and restaurants that were a short drive from town. The town center was alive with tourists and locals who bartered good-humoredly for the crafts and gifts unique to Maui.

The jeep drove around to the rear of the small police station and Jacob got out of the front seat and looked around cautiously, security screening on his own doorstep was a first for him. He gestured to his visitors to go through the blue colored door to the right. Raymond and Sally ducked into the door rather self consciously not sure what to expect, it led to a corridor about twenty feet long. To the left were two rooms with desks and chairs and on their right were two prison cells.

Jacob lead them to the second room "This is my office, which also doubles as an interrogation room," he said, as he entered.

Raymond followed him into the room, it had one small window, one desk and three chairs and very little else. The walls and floor were paneled with wooden planks, which gave the room a warm if not barren feel. A small light bulb hung from the wooden ceiling and one wall held an old map of the island, which somehow gave Raymond the impression that it was way out of date.

Sally entered and Jacob asked, "Anything to drink?"

" No thanks!" They both replied in unison.

Jacob walked over to an aged map limply pinned to the wall and used it to indicate the locations of the main buildings in town, using the jail as a reference point. The International Island Bank was three blocks up to the north.

Raymond was anxious to do something after hours of inactivity. "I think Sally and I should walk around town to get our bearings and scout out an observation post."

"Good idea!" Jacob smiled, "Take your time!" He walked behind his desk and sat down.

Raymond and Sally stepped out the rear and walked cautiously to the Main Street. They felt conspicuous in this new world of intrigue and espionage. At the first corner they stopped to find their bearings, the buildings looked so quaint, with their pastel colored walls and bright white roofs contrasted against the background of a clear blue sky. This was very different from the overcast coldness of the Washington area which they had left barely hours before. They turned right and soon found the Bank at the corner of two intersections. It was a two-story building painted in a pastel yellow color. The window shutters and doors were a dark green, as was the sign above the door with gold letters, written boldly "International Island Bank".

Raymond looked around for a good place to watch for McKenzie but none was immediately obvious. On the opposite corners to the banks were a pharmacy store and two local gift shops. They approached the first gift shop, to the south of the bank entrance, and looked around, stopping to purchase two pairs of sun glasses. It was a small bustling shop and there was no way either of them could stand and watch without drawing attention to themselves. It was the same with the other two stores also.

"This is not good," Raymond confirmed Sally's thoughts.

He looked around for another vantage point; "Looks like we're in trouble…. Let's check out the inside of the bank."

He held Sally's arm and walked over to the entrance. They entered together looking apprehensive and somewhat suspicious, if anyone had been watching them they would have reported them to security.

The interior was a typical bank layout, the room was about fifty feet long and thirty feet wide, three teller's windows immediately to the right, all manned by women, efficiently exchanging traveler's checks for the half a dozen brightly clothed customers. To the left were two unmanned desks and about twenty-five feet down there was an elaborate wooden fence separating the public part of the bank from the private part. Beyond the swinging gate of the fence were two individual offices, both with opaque windows and solid looking doors, giving the comfortable feeling of security. An impressive ceiling, with intricate carved wood panels was suspended about twelve feet above them. The large windows were barred, but allowed sunlight to enter unrestricted giving a light airy appearance to the large room. The front doors, now behind them, were the only obvious entry and exit point, which confirmed Jacob's briefing.

As Raymond gazed around the bank a feeling of futility overcame him, he had until now simply been carried along with the speed of events without rationalizing the chances of success. It had been crazy to think that they could simply fly down to a tourist infested island which was celebrating one of the worlds largest party's and find someone that he could not even remember, but Sally thought she did. He felt foolish at his naivete and anger welled up within him, He was angry with himself more than at anyone else.

He glanced at Sally, her eyes betrayed too that she had come to the same conclusion, then he saw her tense up. She froze, eyes wide and holding her breath, she clutched at Raymond's arm and dragged him towards the nearest teller's window bowing her head self-consciously. Raymond followed her lead a little hesitantly, bemused by her actions. He leaned his head towards her and caught the words.

"It's him!" "It's McKenzie!" she stammered. She clenched his arm so hard her nails cut into his skin but he was oblivious of anything but McKenzie.

He was coming from one of the private offices. "Goodbye," reverberated around the large room the Irish accent was thick. He shook hands with a short balding man, presumably the manager, turned and walked directly towards them. In about five strides McKenzie was through the swing gate and into the public area of the bank and heading purposefully for the door. Dressed in casual gray slacks and a white short sleeved shirt he could have passed for a normal tourist but for the black briefcase he carried in his right hand. His reddish brown hair was cut short and his new feature was a neatly trimmed beard. Before exiting the bank he stopped and put on some sunglasses, then strode out the door, blending in easily with the flow of tourists walking casually down the street.

Sally and Raymond had their backs to him huddled together. She pretended to extract some currency from her purse as if they were about to exchange it. Once the large bank door clicked shut behind McKenzie they turned cautiously and hurried out to follow him.

Raymond and Sally followed him in silence; their feelings of conspicuousness were overwhelming. They separated to dodge other users of the narrow sidewalk, and tried desperately to avoid bringing any attention to themselves. At the edge of the town center, the two story commercial buildings gave way to smaller buildings, and houses. It was obvious they were in the best side of town, the houses were large and well maintained and once belonged to the wealthy ship owners. Their uses now range from summer homes to professional offices. They watched as McKenzie slowed, then turn, he glanced from side to side and went through a small garden gate, up a brick path and into a pink house.

Raymond and Sally looked at each other in astonishment.

"I would not have recognized him if it weren't for his voice" she whispered, "He's changed so much!"

"You did very well," Raymond whispered, his renewed enthusiasm showed in his eyes.

CHAPTER 18

John McKenzie was not born John McKenzie. He never really knew his natural parents. After a brief stay in an orphanage he grew up with foster parents in Hoboken, New Jersey. He remembered little about his formative years, blocked out over a period of time, but felt deep down that they were painful. Independent and self reliant, he never felt as if he fit into his environment. His foster parents Joe and Marge Cirrilo were a kindly couple full of good intentions, but life was indifferent towards them. They had two other older children, Frank and Bobby, who largely resented their adopted brother, John Cirrilo. John always seemed restless and remote, not easily approachable. The common opinion was that he had a chip on his shoulder, but in reality John never understood his moods and neither did anyone else. The effect was very little real communication between John and the family; this gradually led to latent resentment and a deep frustration by all.

John found his companionship in the streets of Hoboken, roaming around in gangs with like-minded youths. The common thread between gang members was a hatred of school, complete disrespect for authority and the need to feel a part of something. The Cirrilos found it easier to let him come and go as he liked and gave up monitoring his attendance at school or rather lack of attendance. The authorities grew increasingly frustrated with his disruptive nature while he was at school and eventually also turned a blind eye on his truancy. John slowly lost his perspective and drifted towards a degenerate life. The only thing Mr. Cirrilo warned him about was that any trouble brought to their door would result in severe consequences. John remembered those words or perhaps the ominous tone of them, but could never really determine what they meant. He did, however, adhere to that one major rule.

Home was a rented two- bedroom apartment much like others in the area. It boasted a lounge, kitchen/dining room and one and a half bathrooms. John shared the bedroom with Frank and Bobby making for very cramped conditions.

Money was always short in the Cirillo household. Joe was an unskilled worker in a small factory nearby, who manufactured picture frames and Marge worked part time in a diner as a waitress. The two wages barely provided for the family, but the diner did supplement the household food requirements. There was a state allowance for fostering John, which helped but he always found himself at the back of the line for pocket money.

At sixteen, like most boys, John became more interested in the opposite sex and needed money to support the habit. This need drove him to take a job in the local Food Hall supermarket. Food Hall was a small supermarket chain specializing in cheap, no nonsense products; modeled on Woolworth's however, its popularity centered around it's liquor store which ensured a steady flow of customers twenty four hours a day. Initially, John collected the shopping carts from around the parking lot, and then graduated to packing the shelves. Sometimes he helped customers to their cars, grateful for the odd tip he might receive, to add to the legal minimum wages of $3.15 per hour. He became less interested in school and persuaded the store manager to gradually increase his working hours. He was considered relatively reliable, although by a low standard, and as help was very difficult to find, the store gladly extended his workdays. The increase in his spending power made him more popular and satisfied his yearning to 'belong' He became the primary source for the gang's cigarettes and even an occasional six pack of Budweiser. The girls found it easy to separate him from his wages and he was often found swaggering in the company of three or four of them, as long as he was spending on the movies, soda, popcorn and candy. It seemed the more he worked, the faster it went and soon as it was gone so were the girls, but he didn't care, at least he felt good some of the time.

At seventeen years of age, John stood about 5'6", wore his brown hair fashionably long and squinted through brown eyes as if he needed glasses. He was not bad looking, but his slightly pointed features, tight lips, and the squint gave him a mean look. The hand me down jeans and shirts were oversized and always looked baggy on his thin frame giving him a malnourished look. He deeply resented the second hand clothes from the older boys, but could never persuade Marge to change this image. Some of the other gang members had similar problems but they just let it roll over their heads, but it irked John constantly.

The gang centered around five people: Chip, Joey, Matt, John, and Carlos, but could easily expand to sixteen. There was never much to do around town and time was wasted away idly on street corners and hanging around the railroad station taunting vagrants. Sometimes John became the entertainment for the others who would gather at the store and tease him when he carried bags of groceries to a customer's car. He hated them for that.

Occasionally the boredom would be replaced by a trip into Manhattan and a walk up from 33rd Street Station to Time Square. This route took them past the drunks and prostitutes who frequently populated 42nd street. The girls looked exciting and a little dangerous, the vibrant noise and bright lights were a magnet for them. Each trip gave them new courage and they soon developed the courage to badger the prostitutes and harass the drug addicts. One warm May evening they took yet another step away from the norms of society

"Yo girl what have you got for me tonight?" Carlos was always the forward one with the girls.

"Go and get your diaper changed" a hard looking eighteen year old girl replied.

"You're missing out," the gang laughed, as he scratched his crotch and they walked towards Broadway.

"Hey man, I just got a fake identity for ten bucks," Joey bragged, flashing a small card

"Let's go and get some beers!" Matt volunteered, there's a liquor store couple of blocks up.

"Some smokes as well!" Chip added," And I mean some Real Smokes!"

The five boys roamed the streets aimlessly, drinking from Budweiser cans hidden in brown paper bags, some smoked Joe Camel cigarettes, some smoked grass, all were loosing their grasp on reality.

Several nights later with nothing to do and no money to do it with, the boys were overcome with boredom. They found themselves outside the store where John worked. It was the anchor development of a small L shaped shopping mall about one hundred yards from the center of town. Food Hall's twenty four-hour service meant shift working three shifts of eight hours each. The day shifts utilized mainly women but the night shift, commencing at 10:00 p.m. was manned only by males, giving the customer an impression of security.

It was 9.45 on a Thursday night and the parking lot was about a quarter full. John and the others stood and scrutinized the activity around the two open cash outs, for about fifteen minutes. They mentally tallied the store's takings.

"I reckon the store takes six hundred dollars per hour, per cash register" Joey noted. "There is probably two thousand in each register right now."

"You're probably right! They will be due to be emptied soon, they do it at around ten each night, just before the night shift comes on!" John added.

They watched as the registers cashed out and the men gradually replaced the women. Discontentment descended on the five youths like a blanket. They stared blankly at the registers,

"Man, what could we do with that money?" Matt asked aimlessly.

"Two guys just made off with five grand from the Food Rite Store in Newark, easy as taking candy from a baby," Carlos quoted a news headline

"Bet we could take three grand from this store!" Matt speculated.

"More like four!" Chip added.

"You wouldn't dare!" Joey challenged them all.

"Who wouldn't?" Carlos almost screamed; his courage had been questioned.

Chip threw his cigarette butt away and said boldly, "Let's do it!"

"Yeah! Lets get rich," Carlos joined in. Bravado replaced maturity in all five now.

"How about Friday night?" Joey sneered.

"Yeah! that suits us fine!" Chip answered for all of them.

They separated, swearing to meet tomorrow at nine p.m. and swaggered home, lost in their own sense of self importance.

Friday passed torturously slowly for John, second thoughts about the robbery consumed him "They'll never do it," he tried to convince himself. " By tonight we'll call the whole thing off, it was a dumb idea anyway!" he thought, his conscience trying to put a brake on his actions. He left his house, at seven p.m. Nervousness had replaced bravado and he was about to return home when he met up with Carlos and together they walked gingerly to the high school. Chip, Joey, Matt and Carlos had not arrived as yet.

"Want a beer?" Pete offered.

"Sounds good to me," Charlie answered taking a can from him.

"You see the Nicks game last night?" Kevin intervened.

"Lousy team, beaten again, they should hire me for a million bucks a game, I could do better!" Pete said confidently.

By the time Chip showed John had visited the bushes twice to relieve himself, nerves had taken control of his bladder.

"Have you seen the new chick at School? Man, she's nice!" Carlos was trying hard to take his mind off his promise to his friends

At nine-o clock Joey and Matt joined the party. Friday night was party night and by 9.30 p.m. the gang, numbered about seventeen. By 9.35 p.m. no one had noticed that the party was five fewer. John and Chip were the first to leave followed by Joey and Matt, then Carlos slipped away to make the 10-minute walk to the strip mall.

"It's busier than last night," Joey observed.

"Yeah maybe too busy," John offered, pointing out the cars, meandering all over in the parking lot, their headlights creating a collage of shadowy figures. Joey and Matt were deadly serious.

"Shut up, you bastards!" Joey spat on the ground, we're going to do this as advertised!" His voice was hoarse.

The others felt trapped, their bravado ebbed away with each step, but they dared not back out, loyalty and courage were on the line.

Joey was speaking now. His voice sounded thick. "The plan is simple. Two of you will cause a disturbance in one of the aisles of the store, the other two will grab the money from the register drawers, I will stand where I can see you all and give the sign!" He looked at them all, his eyes looked glassy and unfocussed. "John, you know the cash drawers best, so you grab the cash. Carlos you're the other grabber." He looked at the store, "Mat and Chip you cause the ruckus!"

The others stood silently their eyes filled with fear, as Joey barked out the orders, as if suddenly graced with leadership and experience. They looked desolate; their faces were gaunt and bloodless. Each wished that someone else would back out. They could not understand how Joey could be so calm, it never occurred to them that drugs had induced Joey's courage. John was fighting a sickly feeling that originated in his stomach and made his head swim, his legs felt weak and from the looks of Carlos he was in a worse condition. They walked towards the store. Joey remained at the entrance while Matt and Chip went straight ahead to the isles holding soda cans and tinned vegetables,

"These will make the most noise!" Chip whispered.

John and Carlos turned right and edged hesitantly closer to the two target cash registers, their gray faces, ashen with fear were an obvious give away, to anyone watching. There was a lull at the cash register near John when Joey gave the sign to Chip and Matt. It all happened so fast that the five teenagers were oblivious of the irreversible paths each of them had just chosen.

The store filled with the crashing sound of tins as a thousand small thunderclaps reverberated throughout the building.

"Help! Help! The shrieks caused panic throughout the store.

The young woman nearest to John leapt up to see what was happening, clutching at the notes she had been counting. Instantly, John jumped toward the open register and scrambled with two hands for the bills lying in the draw, he turned to get out of the store. As he twisted, headlights from a car caught his eye through the shop window and he saw the familiar colors of a police cruiser driving slowly around the parking lot. He stood momentarily stunned, his heart pounding, his legs like lead. Carlos crashed into his immobile body on his way to the exit. John fell to the ground and he heard a woman's voice yelling, "Thief! Thief!"

Carlos ran out of the store, Joey close behind him, Matt and Chip followed.

Customers instinctively ran towards the exit chasing after Carlos. They ignored John, who lay sprawled on the floor amongst a blanket of green bank notes. He looked around in a daze; no one paid any attention to him so he mindlessly scooped up the money and stuffed it into his open shirt. He lifted himself on one knee, and stared at the police cruiser's flashing lights, between a forest of customer's legs. He slowly crawled away from the crowd towards the back of the store. The wail of sirens seemed deafening to him as his senses strained to absorb everything. Panic overcame him and he began to run down the aisles towards the stockroom at the rear of the store. The door was ajar so he let himself into the room and moved through the darkness to the rear door and quietly exited the building. It was a warm night but he felt unusually cold and shivered uncontrollably, his legs would not move. The police sirens continued to fill the air with a cacophony of high-pitched screams, breaking the stillness of the once peaceful night. Irrational fear welled up inside of him and began to run blindly through the streets.

Hoboken railway station loomed out of the darkness as John stumbled to a standstill, the air was sucked from his lungs and he felt dizzy after running for a full twenty minutes; he leaned against a wall gasping in gulps of air. None of his short life had prepared him for this, his mind would not work, his mouth was dry and he was shaking again as his nerves took over his body. He felt sick and his legs seemed useless, he staggered into the station and looked around for someplace to sit and think. The station was empty. New York City commuters had long ago returned to the suburbs, only the homeless and hopeless remained. His head in a fog, he looked up at the sea of destination signs and saw the familiar PATH sign and walked mindlessly in that direction.

"Manhattan would be a good place to hide," he thought, as he stood underground watching for the announcement of the next train on the automatic notice board.

The train rattled into the station five minutes later and he mechanically entered the last carriage and stood alone for the short journey under the Hudson River. At Penn Station he impetuously jumped off and followed the small crowd of passengers through to the main station. The people dissipated into the night, leaving him alone and feeling lost,the depth of these emotions, he had never really experienced before. He stared at the Amtrak departure schedule watching the various destinations clicking into place on the automatic board, together with the departure time and platform number. The first outward bound train was to Boston leaving, in six minutes. On impulse he rushed to the ticket counter pulling some notes out of his shirt.

"One way to Boston" John demanded with a weak voice.

The second class ticket and change was exchanged for a $50 bill and John ran to platform six to join the few people traveling at this late hour. The train rolled slowly into the station, the brakes screeching as it came to a halt. He boarded the train looking pensive, gray, and tired and fell into the first vacant seat he came across. The carriage was empty and he found himself staring blankly out of the window, as the train slowly pulled out of the station. His own hollow eyes stared back at him in pity, reflected by the darkened window. John never moved during the journey northward getting up only as the train slowed into Boston's South Station, just after 2 a.m.

Never having been to Boston previously, he allowed the other passengers to lead him out of the station trying to look inconspicuous and found himself in the heart of Boston's Tramway System, the "T." A deep feeling of hopelessness washed over him, he felt lost again and sat down to wait until his plans caught up with him. He almost forgot about the money that was crushed inside his shirt, now limp and damp with his perspiration.

"I better get somewhere out of sight, and count it," he thought, and looked for a quiet corner.

Suddenly the station reverberated with singing, he looked up to see about ten teenagers strolling down the platform. They were in very good spirits in every sense of the word and made for the platform seat that John was on. Taking John for just another student, they included him in their drunken conversation and before John realized it he was on the last "T" of the night, going to a party at Boston University somewhere along Commonwealth Avenue. The party was a blast, and took his mind off his problems, at least momentarily. He "crashed" at the apartment and woke up the next morning lying on a bedroom floor, with several other bodies. His mouth felt like a sewer and his head exploded in pain. He made his way to the bathroom to relieve himself and wash up. The mirror reflected the fear he felt inside, and he sat on the floor and pulled the money from his shirt. His take, from the store, amounted to a little over six hundred dollars.

"Not damn worth it!" he thought bitterly, as he stared absently at the pile of notes. "I can't believe this!" he muttered to himself and washed cold water over his face to help him think. At least he could pay his way for a while, "How long?" he asked himself.

Fear and apprehension again flooded over him, as he recollected, the events of last night, and he vomited into the sink, until his stomach was drained. He pulled himself together and went to the kitchen and breakfasted with some of his hosts. John was allowed to crash at the apartment until he got fixed up. He used the first fifty dollars of his illegal gains to convince his young landlords that it would be mutually beneficial.

It took John four days to get a job, as a bus boy in an Irish Pub/Restaurant, called *Malones*. His wages were paid in cash avoiding any records and his new duties, mercifully, put his worries on back burner, at least temporarily. Surprisingly, he liked the work and progressed to waiter where his reliability and attitude endeared him to staff and customers alike. His life revolved around the restaurant and he befriended a young Irish American John McKenzie, whose family often came into *Malones*. The two boys were similar ages and had similar interests and they became inseparable.

Mr. McKenzie was in the process of transferring to Ireland with his company and although Cirrilo was disappointed it gave him an idea.

"Let's keep in touch," Cirrilo asked hopefully, as the boys sat in *Malones* drinking an illegal beer during the afternoon break.

"O.K." McKenzie sounded neutral, he was both excited and apprehensive at the prospect of moving to Ireland.

"Gotta pee," McKenzie rose scraping the chair along the floor.

"Have you change for a twenty?" Cirrilo asked.

"Here, take what you want," McKenzie threw his wallet on the table and left for the men's room.

Cirrilo picked up the wallet and ran into the back office. He quickly photocopied McKenzie's social security card and driver's license. The first part of the plan was complete. By the time McKenzie left for Ireland Cirrilo had his friends passport number, credit card numbers and identity.

The day of McKenzies' departure was the rebirth of Cirillo, in the official sense, as Cirrilo adopted McKenzie as his new name, and now had a legitimate passport to his future.

His new identity gave him a renewed outlook on life and he moved to a new apartment, which he shared with two more students. His new co-habitants were studying computer science and their enthusiasm for the subject, inspired John who eventually enrolled in night school for computer programming. Both he and his tutor were pleasantly surprised at his aptitude for the subject. He was a natural. After six months, he was proficient in the common computer languages and his tutor approached him.

"I've set up an interview for you at Global Insurance, no promises but you should go."

"Thanks!" McKenzie held out his hand, a grateful look on his face.

"You'll do o.k. If you keep your head down," the teacher reached out and shook his hand smiling encouragingly.

The interview went well and he was offered a position, initially in a large branch office, several miles north of Boston. He felt very pleased with himself and decided to celebrate by accepting an invitation, by the real McKenzie's, to visit them in Dublin. Aer Lingus were heavily discounting their round trip fares to $299, so John took this unexpected opportunity for a ten-day vacation.

Dublin was fascinating, the Irish people friendly, yet passionately jealous of their heritage. Cirillo became steeped in their culture and absorbed by their politics. His interest in the Irish became an obsession and the highlight of his visit was towards the end when he met some members of the IRA casually in a pub. The discussions were heated and full of passion and made a lasting impression on a person desperate to belong. The new McKenzie returned to Boston full of new thoughts and ideas, his persona invigorated for the first time in his life.

He joined Global and rose rapidly through the ranks and after seven years progressed to second in charge of the Information Services department, headquartered in Boston.

He never forgot his past and often reflected on it bitterly, but it was this suppressed past that drew him towards the IRA ideals and philosophy. His mind became twisted and he felt somehow that he had endured the same injustices as the Irish people.

He was determined to get even with society.

CHAPTER 19

Raymond had no recollection of John McKenzie at all.

"What do we do now?" Sally asked, looking at him quizzically.

Unprepared for any of this Raymond looked lost; he stared at her with unseeing eyes, panic welling up uncontrollably inside of him. A feeling of hopelessness overcame him.

Sally broke the spell by simply asking, "Should I go to the police?"

"Yes, Yes," jumped Raymond, "Get Jacob!" relieved that his inertia had passed. "I'll try to look inside the house," he added without thinking. Raymond glanced at his watch, it showed one fifty, and he felt the mounting pressure as time slipped away, he moved gingerly towards the house.

Sally looked at Raymond momentarily, then glanced towards town, she guessed she was about half a mile from the police station and turned to retrace the route, which lead them here.

Raymond watched her through unfocused eyes as she strode purposefully back toward town; he felt alone and lost as if all hope had left with her. He rubbed his temples to clear his head, then turned his attention to the house. It was a Center Hall colonial. The pink stucco walls formed a startling background for the white window frames giving the impression of a large dollhouse. The front door and screens around the windows were a darker, unrecognizable color. It was flanked on both sides by two smaller houses, neither one was as colorful and could even be described as drab in comparison. The house on the left and farthest away from him seemed unoccupied, and the one to the right was engulfed with light and the sounds of people having a good time.

Raymond carefully made his way past the front of the pink Colonial house and then past the smaller unoccupied blue house, walking as casually as he could. Once past the blue house, he turned right and crept down its side to the small rear garden. He found himself enclosed by lush native bushes and felt fortunate that he was completely hidden from anyone's view. He crept slowly along the back of the blue house concentrating his attention on the faint noises emanating from the adjacent building. Using the cover of rhododendron bushes Raymond moved slowly in the direction of the sounds at the rear of the pink house. A gentle breeze from the North rattled the trees and bushes causing Raymond to pause momentarily. He knelt down then crawled gingerly on all fours to the open kitchen windows, where he heard the rattle of ice cubes on glass. This only heightened the dryness he felt in his own mouth. Slowly he peered in, and immediately saw two men sitting at a large pine table, cocktails in hand. McKenzie's back became visible as he moved towards the men, holding a glass in one hand and a bottle of Bushmill's in the other.

He greeted the two men with his fake Boston Irish accent, "Everything okay?"

"Yes," a second Irish accent responded the clinking of ice drowned out the rest.

"Everything is fine at the bank!" McKenzie stirred his glass with his finger.

"Have you arranged our transport out of here?" the man seemed to slur his words.

"Not yet!" McKenzie fired back.

"Better get on to that!" A third accent, Eastern European Raymond thought, entered the conversation.

"Plenty of time yet!" McKenzie again as he sat down. "You worry too much!"

"I keep alive by worrying too much!" the man barked.

The three men relaxed into a game of five-card stud, the European dealt the first hand.

"Ace high, you're bet," he rasped.

"Five bucks!" An Irish accent responded.

The men chatted idly amongst themselves but Raymond found it difficult to follow the conversation due to their accents and the growing affects of alcohol. Ten minutes passed without event, his legs were now screaming out in pain due to the cramped way he was sitting. He moved positions and fell forward on his hands and knees, the immediate sensation of pins and needles overcame him and he waited until the numbness had gone before moving. He heard live things skittering about the low bushes on either side of him and momentarily froze.

"I hope these are not snakes," he muttered under his breath.

Sweat beaded on his brow at the thought of any reptilian presence and the hair on the back of his neck bristled; strangely enough it was his first thought of fear. His concentration on the discussion lapsed and he became preoccupied with the unseen wildlife. In a quick rush of syllables he caught the name *"Kingfisher,"* instantly he became alert.

The European was talking, "The Kingfisher should be nearing the Avau Channel now."

195

"O.k. O.k." the unknown Irishman interrupted, "just make your bet."

Raymond's senses exploded at the mention of the *Kingfisher* the only vital clue he'd heard for all the pain he experienced. He began to crawl around to the front of the house, anticipating the arrival of Sally and Jacob. No one was there, so Raymond walked towards town and stood out of sight of the pink house.

"This is damn hopeless! We need more help! How many of them are there?" Thoughts bounced around his mind in random fashion and he became preoccupied.

"What's up?" Sally's question startled him.

"Where the hell have you been?" he grilled Sally while looking at Jacob and two police constables.

"Rounding up the cavalry!" she fired back.

"The *Kingfisher* is close by," Raymond blurted out, "someone should notify the coast guard," he instructed, tension clearly in his voice

"Where?" Jacob asked.

"Somewhere in the Avau Channel, I think," Raymond snapped.

Jacob seized the opportunity to avoid trouble and volunteered to contact the coast guard striding off immediately with one constable tagging along behind him.

"There's at least three of them!" Raymond told Sally, a serious tone to his voice.

"Let's see them," Sally said gamely. Her eyes sparkled; she was running on adrenaline now.

Raymond turned to the remaining constable "Stay out of sight, we will be back soon!" He took hold of Sally's arm and duplicated his previous route to the rear of the pink house. As they crept through the bushes this time he smelt the exotic fragrances of orchids and hibiscus his senses heightened as the excitement levels rose within him. He tried to block out the idea of snakes, but nevertheless found himself breathing heavily, he felt his heart pounding loudly and his stomach muscles tight.

The three men were still drinking and playing poker when Raymond and Sally took up their position under the open window. Strangely neither of them felt any sense of real danger from these men, their minds had pushed such logical thoughts dangerously deep into their subconscious's. Raymond sensed that the mood of the men seemed to have changed from one of being relaxed to one of business.

McKenzie was talking. "In addition to the $20 million deposit already paid to your organization we have arranged for $200 million of diamonds to be held for you in Singapore." He paused to take a drink. "As you know the inspection of the goods was satisfactory, so here is the certified letter from Amalgamated Bank indicating the contents and number of the safety deposit box held by them, and here is the key." McKenzie handed the European the key, adding, "The second part of the transaction is complete!"

They all raised their glasses and drank a toast.

"Will the next phase involve Zurich?" the European asked.

McKenzie nodded, silently.

Raymond nearly whistled aloud at the complexity of these arrangements and it explained the reason for the use of so many of Global's bank accounts. He looked at Sally crouched uncomfortably, face looking upward, towards the open window. Her eyes were wide open and lips pressed thin in concentration. Raymond nudged her, pointing that she should follow him, and they both crawled to the front of the house. The Constable showed himself carefully, his eyes were saucer size due to fear. Raymond stood up stiffly and walked across the front garden to him this was a new experience for the young man, and he had conflicting feelings. Danger vied with conscientiousness - conscientiousness won out, for the moment.

"Any movement?" Raymond asked the constable.

"No Sir!'

"Just leave me struggling!" Sally said sharply as she approached them, limping slightly.

"What do you mean?" Raymond was bewildered

"Forget it!" She barked.

Raymond needed time to compose his thoughts and get the cramping sensation out of his legs. He decided to walk back towards town, leaving the nervous young policeman at the house.

"Coming Sally?" he asked, as he moved off.

She screwed her face up, then trailed him down the street. Raymond drew a breath and exhaled slowly, rubbing his cramped legs and said,

"It looks like we were right, this is the final link in a series of transactions, which have already, or will imminently take place!"

Sally nodded silently in agreement.

"They must have consolidated Global's money into regional centers and then transferred the balance to some external account." Raymond stared ahead, not turning his eyes towards her.

"This money was then converted into diamonds for the final transaction." Sally added. "Yes," Raymond walked on. "The concept would be that the millenium bug would disrupt the systems at midnight and would hide, or even destroy, the trail until it was too cold to follow!" He speculated.

"Meanwhile the sellers of the arms are protected, guns for diamonds, avoids any computer problems altogether," Sally finished his trail of thought.

"Clever, very clever!" Raymond whistled in admiration. "These guys may not even be relying on the millennium bug to cover them they may have planted a date virus as insurance - oops, pardon the pun." He grinned sheepishly at Sally.

He noticed the serious look on Sally's face, as reality dawned on her, they were amateurs dealing with professionals and really had little chance of success, she felt helpless and suddenly very very drained.

"What should we do?" she whispered. Her face was desolate

Raymond walked on, without answering. The missing pieces still refused to come together, jumbled in what used to be an analytical mind. Sally followed along quietly, mentally subdued;

She suggested "We should inform Jacob!"

Raymond, still preoccupied, was strangely disturbed by the word "inform", the word floated around in his mind like a kite fluttering in the wind. He suddenly stiffened and drew a deep breath, standing still for a full twenty seconds.

"There must be a radio!" He exhaled. "How were they informed about the transaction? The phones have been unreliable: electronic mail is not working; there must be a radio in that house!" he blurted out, jolting Sally. "How else could they know about the other transaction?"

Raymond's gibberish and preoccupation were frustrating Sally. She looked scornfully at him and asked, "What is the next step?" Not expecting an answer.

"We have to get inside that house and find out what they have in there," Raymond was emphatic. "Let's discuss this with Jacob, I don't think our friends are going anywhere soon."

Raymond strode purposely towards the small police station with Sally following in his wake; she tried to suppress her rising frustration and resentment at Raymond's new found introspectiveness.

At the police station, Jacob listened intently at what his two visitors had to say he was leaning back in his seat at his small desk, fidgeting with a decorative letter opener carved out of whalebone. He was an empathetic listener, but his sympathy ended at their suggestion of raiding the house.

"We cannot enter the house without due cause! As far as we know, they have not broken any of our laws yet!" Jacob stated unexpectedly serious. "All I can do is watch and wait and help the coast guard run down the gun runners. My hands are tied unless these people break our laws." Jacob stood slowly leaned forward placing his two hands on the desk to emphasize his statement.

There was a long lull in the conversation.

Raymond knew instinctively that Jacob was correct, and he did not bother to counter with any argument. He stared at the floor for a moment then looked directly at Sally. They exchanged a conspiratorial look, then he suggested innocently "We should return to the house and simply keep an eye on it."

That's OK! Jacob's smile returned.

Raymond stood up and stretched, then casually made for the door. Sally stood up suddenly stony faced, the chair she was sitting in crashed to the wooden floor, she picked it up, turned and subduedly followed Raymond out of the room. Both strode determinedly out of the police station knowing that it would be they that would be breaking the law soon. They walked in silence towards the pink house each of them feeling lost and empty as they felt the descent back to the reality of the situation. The hustle and bustle of the small town was lost on them as they dodged the mass of colorful bodies already beginning to celebrate New Year's Eve. This should have been one of the happiest days of their lives, but somehow happiness was not one of their utmost thoughts.

The big eyes of the young constable showed relief as he saw the couple approaching, he flashed a large white smile and saluted stiffly. Raymond again asked him to remain out front whilst he and Sally moved to the rear using what was now the usual route. They could hear the slurred voices of the three men as they neared the rear of the pink house; the effect of the drink had turned up their volume and deadened their sense of secrecy. Raymond whispered to Sally that he was going to find a way in and crawled around to the side of the house. He returned within a few minutes he beckoned Sally over to the corner of the house he had just appeared from.

"There's an open window leading to the lounge," he whispered, "It is opposite the dining room where the three men are!"

They reached the window and both peered in.

Between the lounge and the dining room was the flight of stairs leading to the second floor, "The radio will probably be upstairs," Raymond speculated.

Music floated up in the warm scented air accompanied by the sound of laughter from the party next door "This noise would help!" Raymond thought.

He peered into the open window again and noted that it was at the center point of the wall. The furniture was elegant and looked to be styled after Chippendale. To the left of them was a desk and bookcase in front of them a large sofa and two winged chairs upholstered in a coffee colored fabric matching the window treatments. There were two French provincial style side tables and an oval coffee table in front of the sofa. A large threadbare Chinese rug covered the wooden floor. Raymond crawled in silently, Sally, he assumed would remain outside to watch and listen. He was mistaken. Frustrated by her recent exclusion she hoisted herself through the window not waiting for Raymond's approval. They crawled around the well-furnished lounge on all fours heading towards the hallway where Raymond turned and pointed to the sky indicating he was going upstairs.

The men in the dining room were making too much noise to hear them so they made their way quickly up to the landing on the first floor. Raymond scanned the top floor quickly, seeing six white doors contrasted against the pastel yellow walls. Two to his left and four on his right. He motioned to Sally to investigate the two rooms on the left and he started for the nearest door on the right.

The first door he opened led to a small bedroom at the rear of the house, he backed out of the room disinterested. The second door was a linen closet and the third door a bathroom littered with the toiletries of three men. The last door led to a large bedroom facing the street. It had a large bed littered with clothes and papers. The furniture was heavy, mainly pine, and comprised of a wardrobe and dresser. It was obviously occupied by one of the men downstairs but gave no clues as to who during Raymond's brief invasion.

He came back to the landing and walked over the left-hand side rooms just as Sally appeared at the door and waved him in. Just as he suspected there sat the radio and more importantly names, codes, and frequencies.

"Pay dirt," he thought, as he looked over the radio.

Sally searched through the clothes in the room and came to Raymond's shoulder. "McKenzie's room" she whispered.

Raymond was looking intently at the notes and books that were strewn near the American made Kenwood radio when it unexpectedly jumped to life and a metallic voice filled the room. Instinctively Raymond dove at the set and turned down the volume. Shock drained both their faces and they stood ashen as the radio set demanded an answer. Whatever Raymond did would be wrong, if he did not answer there would be a back up procedure put in place and if he did answer he would raise the alarm, indecision momentarily took control, waiting for the adrenaline to kick in. His raw intellect took over and he grabbed the microphone and frequency dial together. Putting on his best Irish accent he began stammering wildly.

"Abort transfer, Abort transfer, d--, danger, --ger," he moved to the microphone back and forward while altering the frequency minutely. The effect he had was better than he could have expected, the listener caught the string of disjointed words transmitted in the panicked voice and let his imagination fill in the gaps

Raymond signed off and shut the power down leaving the caller utterly confused and scared to death. The remaining silence was only broken by Sally's fight for breath brought on by shock. It was like an asthma attack. She tried to suppress the reaction, which only made it worse and heightened their fear and tension. Raymond grabbed whatever paper he could snatch from the tabletop by the radio and dragged Sally by the arm towards the bedroom door.

Footsteps stomping on the bare wooden floors downstairs caused them to jump back into the room. Raymond quickly looked around for a way to escape, fear steadily mounting with the nearing footsteps. There was one window on the side of the room and two at the front of the house. The one at the side lead to a small roof covering a porch and he opened it quickly and jumped blindly onto the roof. He leaned back into the room and dragged Sally bodily through the opening. They scampered along the flat roof to the front of the house, sat down briefly and jumped into the garden at the front and side of the house landing in some fern like bush.

The young police constable stood wide eyed, mouth open, as he watched them land in a crumpled heap and rushed out to help them. They all disappeared towards town before the three men realized that they had had visitors.

Jacob, Raymond and Sally returned to the house fifteen minutes later with three constables to investigate a neighbor's report of a possible break in.

There were no sounds from the house and no one answered the door. Two constables were sent around the rear of the house while Jacob and the other entered the front. Jacob shouted "Police officers!" Mimicking the celluloid detectives of the movies, then strode inside confidently. The house was empty, the only signs of habitation remaining were those of a very hasty exit, clothes strewn everywhere, drinks spilled and cases and equipment left.

When Raymond and Sally entered, Jacob turned to face them and said, "Looks like our pigeons have flown the coup!" He waved towards the recently vacated rooms.

This is not how Raymond envisaged the end of this assignment and looked desolate, his all day marathon had yielded less than menial results and he felt cheated and looked drained

Sally looked a little more self satisfied and said with a cheeky smile.

"Not quite!" She held up five passports, which she had taken from the bedrooms, Raymond inspected the documents, "Two look genuine but three are forgeries."

"At least McKenzie and Company may be arrested for something after all," Jacob beamed.

"We can be thankful for small mercies," Sally intervened.

Jacob laughed aloud and instructed his men to search the house.

CHAPTER 20

Kishwar Jaheel, the Indian Secretary General of the United Nations had retained her hauntingly beautiful appearance despite the daunting responsibilities of her prestigious office. She did not look her forty-nine years, due mainly to her delicate facial features and almost perfect complexion. She had piercing black eyes and long silky black hair flowing below her shoulders. Her petite figure, standing five foot four inches, gave a deceptive image belaying her toughness and determination. To supplement her high IQ she had developed an extraordinary intuition, which rarely failed her. She was at her desk in New York when the President's call came through.

"What do I owe this pleasure John?" she immediately smiled into the telephone. Her almost perfect teeth were on display now. She and the President had worked closely for about five years and were closely aligned on most issues and philosophies.

The President sensed her smile and found himself smiling also.

"I'm afraid it's not a social call Kishwar," President Alexander said. "Damn nuisance on the biggest night in one thousand years, eh!" He paused.

"May I start with a question first?" Alexander continued. "Have you heard about any unusual incidences occurring around Asia Pacific tonight?"

"No nothing which would be construed as abnormal," Kishwar replied, "but we have had difficulties with our E mail systems and our telephones. I put that down to excessive exuberance. It will be difficult for some people to miss the world's largest party."

"Yes, I know what you mean and those are some of the problems I am having. I thought I would share them with you so here goes." Alexander said somberly. "Mixed in with our normal intelligence reports earlier today we have had notification of accidents and incidents which in isolation would appear random in nature. A young operative became curious and made a convincing case that these events could be attributed to the failure of computer systems to recognize the year 2000. We have all heard about the build up about this issue and assumed it was under control. To a large extent this is true, the vast numbers of systems are compliant, however, some are not for many, many reasons. The problem is that if the non-compliant systems pass dates to the compliant ones we may have problems. The example, I understand, is if we are 99% compliant how much of the remaining bad 1% will affect the good 99%. This is a simplistic view! You catch my train of thought? He paused.

"Yes I do John," she said.

"It's like a virus, one bad cell introduced into the body attacks the good cells aggressively until checked." The analogy pleased him, bringing a human concept to all of this technology.

"The large systems we use around the Globe are like our organs keeping the body functioning and growing." He continued, "The networks are like the arteries and veins carrying the good cells and sometimes the bad cells to the organs."

"We may be experiencing a few bad cells in our blood stream without recognizing it." Alexander's strong oratory skills were on display now. "But left unchecked this could be a highly contagious problem."

Kishwar remained silent, as her intuition prepared her for the worst.

"Our intelligence also picked upon on an elaborate electronic robbery of Global Insurance Inc., which seems dependent on the success of this millennium bug to collapse world systems and cover their crime. "This theft, we think, is also linked to gun running and terrorists and we are investigating this thoroughly," Alexander paused for effect and then continued, "We also picked up troop movements on the Iraq Kuwait border but think this is unrelated for the moment." He paused again. "We have sent two of our phantom IV's out to observe, and will keep you posted."

"Am I going too fast? Alexander hesitated.

"No, not at all John, unfortunately my mind is racing ahead!"

Alexander continued. "These events prompted me to hold a meeting with my staff who reluctantly confirmed that our conclusions could be realistic. We identified possible problems, then decided to form a central response team to help the country through any crisis. My staff thinks that the United States is in a leadership position on this so I thought I would bring you up to date."

Kishwar broke her thoughtful silence.

"Contingency plans are always advisable John but do you think there will be lives threatened?" Her intuition led her to the insightful question.

"Our meeting suggested that power generation shut down could be catastrophic as would runaway nuclear reactors. The microchips, controlling equipment in some plants may have been overlooked. There's just no telling! In fact nothing is predictable and that's part of the problem." Alexander made the statement seem like a threat.

"Why do you think we have not heard anything yet from the countries who have already experienced the date change?" Kishwar asked.

"Too early for anyone to recognize a link, or communications are not up to snuff. Even the fact that it is a weekend will have an affect." Alexander responded.

"Any suggestions John?"

"You could survey the countries that you can contact exchange relevant information." His suggestion was weak, but all he could think of.

"I'm considering declaring a state of emergency so that people will remain at home at least for Saturday and Sunday, Alexander added. "It's lucky, or God's will, that we have a weekend to react." He paused, "The trouble with this situation is if we do nothing, whatever happens we will be pilloried and if we take action and cause panic, ditto."

"It's a difficult call," Kishwar thought aloud.

"Yes, my sentiments exactly, we really need more input, but time is against us."

Kishwar was pensive, but had already decided whom to contact and was itching to get on with it now.

"John I'll get right to it and let you know as soon as possible what happens," she replaced the phone saying. "Thanks for your call."

The two leaders stared at their cradled telephones momentarily lost in similar thoughts.

The first call Kishwar made was to Prime Minister Baird in London. For two years he had warned the U.K. and Europe about the economic consequences of the millennium computer bug. He had appealed mainly to the business community warning of world recession unless the problem was taken seriously. He was not available immediately, but one of his aides promised a prompt reply.

She then called Herr Schmidt, the German Chancellor who was in, but could not give her any real input, however, promised that he would review the matter immediately.

The French Premier, Henry Disdain dismissed the issue without much thought. However, as a nation more dependent on nuclear power than most he immediately contacted his minister of power and industry, Charles Dupre, for an update.

"Charles, I have just been contacted by The Secretary General of the United Nations about the millennium crises. She has heard about problems in various countries. What is the status of Superpheonix?"

Charles was caught unawares, he hesitated then began to ramble. "As you know Henry the Superpheonix is the largest and most advanced reactor in the world. Our teams in Creys Malville have been working for a year to decommission this fast breed reactor." He was playing for time. "You just do not close it down like you shut down a bakery."

Henry Disdain became irritable; "Get to the point quickly Charles," he said brusquely.

"Fast Breeders use sodium as a cooling agent, instead of water, which slows down the neutrons fired at the fuel. That makes the plants more powerful and allows them to create more plutonium than they consume, effectively breeding their own fuel. All this is computer controlled. At midnight the controls became ineffective for some unknown reason and we have an incident at the site. Local experts think they can contain the problem." Dupre exhaled slowly.

There was a long silence. Disdain felt rage rising inside him, "Keep on top of this Charles and brief me every hour, without fail," he slammed the phone down and cursed under his breath.

Kishwar's call to the Japanese Prime Minister and Russian President did not get through.

The Canadian President, Patrick Stewart, was well aware of the issue and agreed with Alexander's position.

Signor Perez of Mexico did not think that Mexico would be vulnerable to the problem except perhaps some downtime in the telephone systems.

Kishwar sat back after 45 minutes and did not feel very confident about her quick survey and took a mental note.

"3 votes suggesting problems assuming UK concurred.

2 votes for no real issues

1 vote unclear"

The telephone disturbed her thoughts and she picked up to find Jack Baird on the line.

"Thank you for returning my call." She said.

"A pleasure ma'am!" Baird's voice was polished with little accent.

Kishwar related her previous conversations ending with, "My straw poll was not very encouraging I'm afraid."

"Well ma'am my vote would be on the problem side," Baird said solemnly.

"We have been fortunate that we retrained twenty thousand people in anticipation of problems. Also we have four days to identify issues before the country returns to work."

"Have you any specific plans?" Kishwar asked.

"We have organized a small central response team to try and co-ordinate efforts."

"Yes, the USA is doing the same," Kishwar said evenly.

"Will you be able to help other countries?" She added.

Baird hesitated, collecting his thoughts, finally he began, "Of course, we will do what we can."

Kishwar sensed his reluctance; "Do you foresee any other issues, Prime Minister?"

"Unfortunately I do," Baird said emphatically. "I firmly believe that the Y2K problem will put intense pressure on the European monetary union. The common economic policy will not cope with the different ways this problem will affect the individual economies. It is too new a union to cope with this kind of pressure so soon."

"What makes you think this?" Kishwar was concerned.

"Well, I'm sure you got different responses to your questions about the Y2K, from Germany, France and the U.K?"

"Yes, that is correct," Kishwar confirmed.

"Each country has a different perspective on the problem and each country concentrated on its own priority. The EMU conversion work was similar in size to the Y2K effort." Baird hesitated. "Those countries entering the EMU concentrated on that project, to the detriment of the Y2K, therefore I think some countries may face larger problems than they currently anticipate."

"I hope I am wrong in this" Baird added without conviction.

Kishwar sighed audibly, the silence became awkward and Baird felt he had to defend his position.

"The slow down of cross border cash flows due to either EMU or Y2K computer problems will cause chaos. It does not matter why it occurs only that it has a good probability to occur. My guess is that the projects were too large and too complicated to be tackled concurrently."

Kishwar appreciated his opinion but did not want to face the consequences.

Baird continued, "In a period when less integration of systems was safer we took the decision to become centralized."

"Thank you for your input" Kishwar needed time to think, after all it was just one opinion. She began to sense why countries had different perceptions of the problem.

One thing was certain, she was proposing a central resource.

She called the White House and updated Alexander on the developments.

CHAPTER 21

Jon sat in his apartment anxiously waiting for the police or the Australian National Security agency, ANS, to contact him. He made coffee, tried to read yesterday's newspapers, and paced the floor of the now empty apartment. The remaining guests from last night's party had left to nurse their first hangovers of the new millennium. The rooms smelled of smoke and stale beer, but Jon made no effort to clean up. The open windows had no effect on the staleness which hung over the rooms like a fog, exacerbated by the presence of half empty beer cans still littering the place.

The waiting and the atmosphere of the apartment depressed him so he went outside and paced the sidewalk. His thoughts drifted back to his childhood in the USA. In particular Sam, who helped him escape his fate, and Maria who introduced him to sex. It was a long time since he reminisced and it brought a smile to his face.

Still no police. He became agitated

He sat on his Norton Dominator and casually inspected the light alloy cylinder head and dusted imaginary dirt from the silver paintwork on the tank and featherbed frame. Time passed slowly, he started the bike, revving the twin cylinder engine, and listened to the familiar powerful roar. Pushing the 400-pound bike off of its stand he drove slowly down the street, keeping an eye on his apartment for his expected visitors. It felt good after the confines of the apartment. The light breeze invigorated him; the sun brightened his somewhat stale outlook on life. The engine purred effortlessly as he drove past his apartment again and Jon had the urge to open the bike up. Impulsively he turned left at the cross street and headed down to the sea front, left again and he was driving parallel to the sea watching the sun glint off of the dark blue sparkling surface. A few miles along the coast road he turned left again and then made purposefully for Dock Road.

"To hell with the police!" He thought.

His second trip was much easier and he reached the street in fifteen minutes. He stood the bike up in the same place as before, and looked toward apartment 1a. The apartment looked quiet, there was no movement in the street at all, everyone was lying low recovering from whatever, poison took their fancy the evening before.

Jon went round to the rear of the building again and crept up to the same window, cautiously peering inside. In the back of his mind he thought that he should be certified as insane, but the excitement had become a drug to him and he felt more alive than he had for some time.

The bed remained unmade, but the clothes were gone, the window was still open. He strained his ears for any stray sounds but could not hear a thing; his intuition sensed no one was home and without hesitation he put his hands on the windowsill and hoisted himself head first through the opening, landing quietly on the floor.

He slowly opened the door and looked into the kitchen, the scene of his previous mistake. Still no sounds, he turned right and crept into the front room, no one there. Fear involuntarily swept over him as images of the struggle permeated his mind and he rushed to check out the kitchen and bathroom. Only the knotted tights and curtain remained of those images and he relaxed a little as he scanned the other rooms.

Nothing much of interest caught his eye, so he strode back to the front room again. It was much the same a before however, with less clutter, as if something was missing. He went over to the radio and searched for anything that looked like a clue. The radio was dead as expected as he still had the fuse in his pocket. He remembered the computer and glanced over to where it had been.

"Shit," he thought, "I should have taken that with me!"

The note pad he previously looked at was still there but blank pages stared back at him. Not even the old gumshoe trick of looking for pen imprints yielded any clues. Feeling disheartened he went back into the bedroom and looked around again. The wardrobe was full of clothes, both men and women's, that questioned his original assumption that the couple had fled. He started to search the mans clothes methodically but only turned up receipts for dry cleaning and groceries. The woman's clothes yielded even less. He searched the dresser without success and picked up the scattered debris on the floor.

A woman's magazine lay on the bedside table and he picked it up, something slipped out of the pages and slid under the bed. Jon dropped to one knee to recover it and just caught a glimpse of a woman's purse. A dark brown leather bag about six inches by nine inches with leather straps. He stretched to recover it dragging it over the floor with his fingertips. Sitting on the bed he opened the purse and was startled by its contents; the largest article was a snubbed nose automatic pistol about seven inches long. "Berretta,' he noted the name on the handle. Jon froze at the realization of danger and shivered involuntarily at his last chillingly close call. The bag also contained a wad of Australian currency, cosmetics, and some hand written messages. The notes took his mind off of the gun and he laid it on the bed. One note caught his attention it was in Gaelic, an obvious giveaway now. Jon was delighted and put everything back into the bag and made his way to the window. He put one leg outside and was concentrating on the other leg when something hit him on the head. It was a strange sensation; he felt the blow but no immediate pain as he struggled out of the window. A second punch to the kidneys dropped him to the floor inside the room; the purse fell into the yard. Hands mauled him as he tried to struggle free. The pain in his head exploded as the delayed effects of the blow stabbed at his senses. He felt his body being kicked and winced at the pain but instead of subduing him the pain stirred his sense of survival. Suppressing a curse he tried to deal with this torture, as a black leather shoe came into his restricted field of vision. He felt a warm sticky liquid running down the side of his face as a foot disengaged his head. He looked just in time to see the shoe draw back to repeat the punishment. Instinctively both hands grabbed at the foot and heaved. The unbalanced figure crashed to the floor letting out a gasping curse of pain. The body lay motionless and fighting for breath. Jon lunged at the prone figure throwing a punch to his assailant's face at the same time. There was a sickening crack as bone hit bone and Jon landed on the unmoving body.

He screamed knowing that his fist was a mass of shattered bone and flesh. He could not fight on and rolled off his assailant blinded by the pain he felt in his head, back and hand.

He lay there for several seconds, waiting for, and fearing the worst, eventually he realized that his opponent must be equally hurt. Nothing happened in the deadly stillness. Pain tore at his senses and blood was trickling into his eyes as he tried to move, he had never felt like this before as pain vied with a sense of survival. The sense of survival was slowly winning. Using the bed as a crutch he managed to get to a kneeling position and looked at the still body of Patrick Kelly.

His lower jaw was in an unnatural position and his nose was just a bloody mass of flesh. Jon was relieved to see the shallow movement of his chest as Kelly's lungs searched for air.

It took Jon an additional five minutes to call the police and twelve minutes for them to arrive. During that twelve minutes Jon realized that the story he had to tell would probably ensure his extended stay in a psychiatric hospital.

His only hope was Raymond Bennett. He rushed into the front room, fumbling for the fuse, he took out in his previous visit, called Tom Ricer and left a bizarre sounding message on his recorder. Just before he heard the noise of police sirens closing in on Dock Street.

CHAPTER 22

Kishwar was lost in thought at the magnitude of the issues caused by the millennium bug. The project had been a windfall for her native country whose talents were used extensively in the reprogramming efforts. India's gross domestic product had shown spectacular growth in the three years leading up to the present, as the world utilized the vast computer talent hidden within the country's borders. India's schools had been turning out thousands and thousands of top class software engineers annually to cope with the brief but overwhelming demand to reprogram the old software systems to comply with dates in the new millenium.

Satellite dishes dotted the skylines of Mumbai, Madras, Bangalore and many other cities, as India became the world center for software remediation and development.

"What had gone wrong?" she asked herself. It was a question she had no desire to face, "What was the right thing to do? Should she use her well developed intuition or follow her rational thoughts through these uncharted waters?"

The telephone rudely interrupted her train of thought. She picked up the phone and said "hello!"

Herr Schmidt was fulfilling his promise to return her call having made some inquiries himself. "I'm afraid I'm not too hopeful about the situation." Schmidt got straight to the point. "I've been told that the resources needed to complete the EMU conversion and then the Millennium effort were insufficient." I am uncertain as to the consequences but think there may be the following possibilities.

1. Business systems may not support normal transactions and companies will be unable to take and deliver orders, or pay and receive cash. This may paralyze industry after a short while and even bankrupt weaker companies.

2. Government systems may restrict movement of goods if import and duty systems collapse. Certainly Air Traffic Control failure may limit some commerce.

3. The micro-control of equipment may close down transport, bridges, shipping, factories, heating, power petroleum, etc.,

Banking and money transfers could be erratic." Schmidt took a breath then continued. "We have some contingency plans to help with the flow of goods but have left it to business to cope with the majority of issues. It is also a weekend which helps in some respects, but may complicate the decision making process if key people are inaccessible."

Kishwar listened intently, "Do you have any prioritization effort defined?"

" No! None have been defined yet!"

"What do you think will be your greatest challenges?"

"In this cold weather heating could be a short-term problem. We're not sure about the reliability of our communication systems." Schmidt was reflective.

"I assume the general public is unaware?" Kishwar queried.

"Yes and no. They know there may be some disruption, but not necessarily how much or how bad. Since we do not know what will happen it is difficult for us to warn the public" His German logic was impeccable as usual.

"Have you contacted any other countries about this?"

"No" he almost whispered. "There has been an almost universal fear of making this public."

"Can you provide support to other countries if needed?" Kishwar again.

"That is difficult to answer Madam.... But we would certainly try!"

"Do you have any plan?" he asked.

"Not yet but the Americans have began to organize a central response team and we should consider the same."

"JA! JA!" Schmidt thought aloud, instinctively using his native tongue as his stress level increased.

Kishwar thanked Herr Schmidt, asked where he could be contacted throughout the night and put the receiver down. "There's just no time!" she thought biting her lip hard without releasing it.

She called President Alexander again and updated him about Schmidt's thoughts.

Alexander said that they were now redirecting all naval ships to the major cities at risk with sub freezing weather. "Anchorage and Nome, Alaska, Boston and Seattle for starters." He highlighted. "These ships will standby for any emergencies and act as communication centers if the need occurs." He took a shallow breath.

"Have you solved the communication problem yet?" She inquired.

" No! Not really! We are sending the AWAC planes up non-stop to replace any satellite failures, which we think will be limited," he sounded uncertain. "Our National Guard has been placed on alert to assist in anything major and all other military services have been told to stand by." Alexander said he hoped this would be unnecessary but prudence was the best precaution. "The major issue will be the collapse of communication, if we don't know what's happening we cannot redirect resources."

"Mmm. The same issue that Herr Schmidt mentioned." She thought.

Alexander was at a loss for contingency plans on this count. "We have realigned our Geosats to photograph major dams, power stations, and bridges just to monitor any problems. I intend to make use of the emergency broadcast system to inform the public as soon as I have verification that our strategy is working."

Kishwar was taking notes and mentally noted that not only was the USA most prepared but as usual they have the most resources. How could China and India possibly prepare for this?" She asked herself.

"Incidentally I have redirected a small task force to answer the IRAQUI threat, I hope it is not needed." Alexander did not feel or sound confident on this matter.

After the conversation with Alexander, Kishwar called in her assistant and drafted a communiqué to be sent to as many Premiers as possible.

It read: "Millennium computer Bug Advisory.

Some countries are experiencing severe problems due to the above and others are anticipating problems. Action taken varied by country but summarized as follows:

1. Naval ships deployed to act as refugee centers in freezing coastal areas.

2. Military support organized to assist in catastrophic circumstances.

3. Alternative communication systems deployed.

4. General public to be informed.

Please let me have your response and notification of any problems."

This message was sent out via voice, electronic mail and radio to ensure the best chance of receipt. Communications with Europe were beginning to break down.

Baird was the first to reply. "Agree with actions noted. We have deployed royal Navy also for communications and we have employed the 'neighbor system'. Each town has to contact its nearest neighbor and pass back down the line any breakdown in communication after midnight. All forces are on stand by."

Premier Disdain faxed a reply. "France concentrated their efforts on their nuclear power stations; we are experiencing some slight problems with one reactor but should have it under control soon. We also deployed troops to ski areas in case of power failures."

The messages from Germany, Italy, Spain, and Scandinavia were never received in the U.S.A.

The United Nations Office in New York became a frenzy of activity as people were redeployed to make contact with Europe. The people at A.T.&T. were contacted and were frantically working to resolve the issue. They had experienced a network breakdown in April 1998 and were the best prepared for back up systems. However there was still no contact as yet.

Kishwar telephoned Alexander. "We've lost contact with Europe John," she said tentatively.

"Yes, I know." The President said, almost reluctantly. "My people have suggested we redeploy our fleet across the Atlantic to act as relay beacons for communications...it seems rather archaic but it's all we can offer under the circumstances? He sounded depressed. "I've given the order and will keep you informed," the President signed off.

CHAPTER 23

Six tired and disheartened people began to search the house; Raymond and Sally remained downstairs while the police searched upstairs. It was a half-hearted search and yielded very little new information. They found a note, which confirmed the name of the ship carrying the last part of the arms delivery as *Kingfisher,* and gave the contact names for the International Island Bank, as John McKenzie and Patrick O'Dell.

The small group gravitated to the kitchen, Raymond turned to Jacob, "I think the Bank Manager should be officially informed of any potential fraudulent transfer of funds."

Jacob picked up the telephone, "It's dead," he shrugged his shoulders as he replaced the receiver. "I'll drive over and have a word with him" he said, "I'll leave the two constables here with you, to be on the safe side. It's unlikely that anyone will return, so make yourselves at home."

He left through the front door accompanied by a constable. He instructed the other two constables to watch the front and rear door until relieved.

Sally felt tired but needed something to do to take her mind off the disappointment. She automatically began tidying the kitchen; Raymond watched her for a moment, then searched for some glasses, to pour a well-needed drink for her.

He found two clean glasses in a kitchen cabinet then looked for some alcohol. He vaguely recollected that the dining room had been the last place where he had heard the clink of glasses and he walked over to the formal table. The remnants of a meal still adorned the table together with a half-finished bottle of Island rum, some Bush Mills Irish whiskey, and some playing cards. The whiskey looked good to him and he poured three fingers into each glass. Returning to the kitchen he topped it up with water and added ice cubes. The two last acts would have guaranteed his immediate demise had any Irishmen been present, he mused.

Raymond returned and reached to offer her the drink, and they stood in the center of the kitchen sipping their whiskey quietly.

"Not exactly the U.S. fifth Cavalry eh?" Raymond broke the silence. "I don't know how I expected to this to turn out but this is not it."

Sally looked exhausted "No I guess it did not end the way I expected either but look on the bright side we'll be sleeping in beds tonight."

A smile crept over Raymond's face; he took a gulp of whiskey and held out his hand. "That's right! care to choose one Madam?"

Sally reached for his hand and gently lead him to the stairs. The softness of her touch ignited something inside of him and they tip toed upwards leading each other through the bedrooms to make a joint choice. Again they found themselves in McKenzies bedroom.

Raymond was drawn to the radio; he switched it on absent-mindedly. His brow beaded with perspiration as he recollected their last encounter with the set. "I should call Australia" he turned to Sally, "just to see what happened there."

She nodded her approval as she lay on the bed.

He put down his drink beside the Kenwood Radio, and selected the HF Band, and started calling Australia.

He tried for five or six minutes without result, then on an impulse called New Caledonia. Tom Ricer answered wearily, the first day of the millennium had exhausted him and he was ready to catch some zzzz's.

"Tom? Raymond Bennett here!"

"Hi Raymond," the sounds literally crawled over the airwaves and reached Lahaina in a lazy mood.

"I've tried to get through to Jon but cannot raise him!"

"Try the Sydney police" Tom butted in. "Got the Goddamn strangest call from him some time back, sounded like he was in a great deal of pain and one step ahead of the fuzz!"

"Hell! what did he do?"

"I think he caught up with the bad guys or they caught up with him, either way he did not sound in good shape."

"How can we find out?"

"Probably the best way is to get your diplomats to talk to their diplomats and in a year or so you might know what happened!"

Tom's caustic comment was closer to the truth than Raymond wanted to think about. "God, I'll have to do something," Raymond thought aloud.

"Well get your operatives to find out," Tom was too tired for this.

"O.K! O.K!" Raymond said sharply, "By the way we spoiled the transaction on this end."

"Really!" Tom was more alert now.

"Catch the bad guys?"

"Not quite" Raymond said reluctantly, his tone betrayed his disappointment. "But we got the money and their passports, which should make life more difficult for them."

"Chalk one up for the good guys!" Tom was tired again.

"I'll talk to you soon." Raymond signed off.

He looked over at Sally lying on the bed, she looked very enticing, a playful expression on her face, her head propped up by one arm, her blond hair loose and careless, as she watched him. His thoughts turned to pleasure as he anticipated the next hour's activity. On impulse he made another call to leave a status report with Al Pagano and to try and find out what happened to Jon.

Pagano was unavailable but the communications operative promised him that he would pass the message on to him as soon as possible. Raymond signed off. His lips curled into a smile as he anticipated the next hour or so.

He turned lovingly to Sally but the excitement rising within him was crushed when he saw that she was now sound asleep. He stood up and paced the small room; he could not shake his sense of failure and frustration. He looked out of the window where he and Sally had escaped. A heavy fragrance filled the air and he relaxed and sent over to the bed. He lay down beside Sally and dozed off as well.

The dream was exquisite with Sally gasping his name as they enjoyed each other's bodies. The words "Raymond! Raymond!" drifted lazily through his mind.

"Raymond Bennett" it was more harsh now "Bennett where are you? This is the White House, come in!"

"Hell! It's the radio," his thoughts scrambled as he fought against layer upon layer of sleep. His mind was still asleep. The radio crackled again demanding an answer. "Bennett come in?"

Raymond tumbled from the bed and grabbed the microphone; "What, what do you want?"

The disembodied voice seemed tin like. "I've got Mr. Pagano on for you, you ready?"

"Ugh, eh yeah, yeah, put him on!" he spluttered groggily, his mouth dry.

"Pagano here!" the set shouted at him making him wince slightly. It was obvious Pagano was not used to using HF radio "Got your message about the transaction, good work!" He paused.

"When this 2,000 thing is over we'll mop up the culprits," he paused again, the message was staccato like. "I've got John Sloan and the President who want to thank you for your good work," Pagano continued. "Hold on."

Raymond fought the rising sickness and felt the sharp taste of the Bush Mills for the second time. This conversation was unexpected and he was not prepared for it.

In true character Pagano had involved Raymond when he thought that the mission was a failure and used all his skill to subtly shift the blame by praising Raymond's unlucky efforts, however the plan had back fired. The President was delighted by the outcome and that there would be no political ramifications and extradition orders to manage. On top of that the arms and money did not change hands in American jurisdiction. The coast guard had warned off the *Kingfisher,* thus avoiding any trouble. A political win all round.

It was a delighted President Alexander who spoke. "Son, I want to thank you on behalf of the American people for your dedication, ingenuity and sheer guts in following this thing through. It's people like you who make America great." His oratory skills were motivational and Raymond felt good again. "How are you feeling?" He added.

"Fine, just fine Sir." Raymond lied. "However, I didn't do it alone," Raymond stuttered.

"I know son, but if you did not pull this thing together, no saying what would have happened. How did you cotton on to it?"

"It was a friend of mine in Australia who put two and two together and when we discussed it over the radio we just thought alike and the pieces fit," Raymond said flatly.

"Well whatever happened, great work!" The airwaves went silent.

"Now f only you could solve our next problem?" Alexander muttered subconsciously.

"What's that sir?" Raymond's brow furrowed deeply and he wished he had not asked the question.

"This millennium bug is causing communication problems throughout the world and we don't have a way to collect and disseminate data reliably! Any ideas?" The President sounded condescending; his experts had been working on this issue for several hours without result.

"Yes Sir" Raymond replied, enthusiasm reentered his psyche.

"Really!"

"Yes Sir! You're using it."

"What?" Alexander barked.

"The HAM Radio network," Raymond paused, "It's worldwide and they tend to help in local emergencies, no reason why they can't do it globally."

"Are you serious?" demanded the President.

"Yes sir!" There are over half a million Hams in the USA alone they use HF, VHF and UHF to communicate wherever and whenever they want. They have their own satellites and some of them can even communicate in Morse code. They are your best global network resource available under the circumstances."

A General at the Presidents side was nodding subtly in agreement embarrassed that this fact had slipped by everyone. The President was flabbergasted.

"I can't thank you enough son!" He growled more at his staff than at Raymond. "Now I'll have to go to see how we use this god sent resource."

"Just one thing Sir" Raymond ventured sensing that he had just solved the President's heartburn.

"Yes Son!" the President barked through the radio set

"This Australian colleague Sir, the one I mentioned to you previously, he's been arrested by the Sydney Police. Is there anything you could do for him? His name is Jon David!" He pressed his luck.

"Get the details to me and I'll handle it, it's the least I can do." The sentiment was that this conversation was now over and the airwaves went silent.

Raymond sat in a dream like trance staring at the set. It was Sally's voice that brought him back to reality. He turned around and looked at the indentation on the pillow where her head had been, he frowned

"Where are you?" he called out.

"Right here!" she was behind him slowly climbing out of her dress, a playful expression on her face.

Raymond stood up and turned to face her, she saw his pants bulge and smiled wickedly. She looked flawless, as she came to him dressed only in a black lace bra and panties, her hands loosened his shirt buttons slowly rolling it off his broad shoulders, revealing a solidly muscled torso tapering to narrow hips. She moved to his belt and tantalizingly loosened it. Raymond was wild with desire but showed no sign of emotion. His pants were around his ankles now, he looked into her eyes and started to speak but no words came. She stood on her toes and gently felt for his lips with hers. Raymond was surprised at the strength of his feelings for Sally. He truly loved her and wanted to be with her,......always.

They were locked inside each other's feelings, as they embraced fiercely, frantically searching out each other's pleasure points.

CHAPTER 24

The President felt a mixture of elation and anger after speaking to Raymond. Elation that there was a network which could report on local conditions within the U.S.A. and for that matter other countries also. Anger that his advisors overlooked this simple solution.

"Damn bureaucrats are not happy unless answers are complicated or convoluted! How many times do we overlook the obvious?" he thought. His mood was black now.

Not one of his entourage was volunteering to break his mood, they all favored the safety of silence as they followed in line back to the oval office.

"Well it looks as if we've got some feet on the ground already," the President made it a statement "Now you all tell me how we can use it effectively." He glowered scornfully at the dozen or so self-conscious faces in front of him.

"I'll inform the Secretary General of the UN that we may have a potential communication strategy that will see us through the initial stages of this blasted menace." He turned towards the telephone; this act in itself dismissed the group summarily.

The staff all scattered as the President reached for the telephone, they were relieved the pressure was over at least temporarily.

President Alexander was immediately connected to Kishwar and they dropped the preamble. Kishwar was skeptical at first, not being familiar with the concept of HAM radios but found Alexander's argument convincing. The only problem they both could foresee was the military's reluctance to concede that this amateur network was preferable to theirs. The real answer was that every system and operator would have to be used to even begin to have an effect on this issue. But no one should underestimate the influence of misplaced egos and the incorporation of the amateur status into professional ranks. The two heads of state debated the good intentions of amateurs versus the sheer egocentric selfishness of professionalism.

During this debate the President had mentally decided to use Raymond to help spread the word via the HAM network, "At least some of the amateurs would get the correct message," he thought to himself.

"Madam I will leave it to you to get clearance from the other heads of state but remember once we set the ball rolling these operators know no boundaries! No border or politics or ethnic barriers will stop them!" He warned.

"That's what I'm afraid of" Kishwar said, "At least we should begin with a written script to ensure early consistency. We will lose it soon enough in translation."

"A good idea," Alexander agreed, "I'll get my spin-doctors to draft one and get it to you." After the first half dozen messages I doubt if anyone will understand what it is about, but I can't think of anything else," he said solemnly. "At least in the United States we will verify the message via our national warning system!" Alexander was anxious to start the chain now.

"We'll have to give these people designated centers to contact!" Kishwar added hastily.

"Yes! You're right!"

Kishwar knew she did not have time for consensus and decided to send another mass communique via voice, e-mail and fax. Once the ham radio operators united, each government would have to react internally, as they saw fit. The political risk was great but nothing compared to the potential loss of lives.

True to his word, President Alexander had the first draft of the proposed communique ready for discussion and faxed it to Kishwar. The fax spit the brief message out:

"To: The Ham Radio community

Re: The year 2,000 computer problem

From: President Alexander

Early programming work in computer systems used two digits for the year in any date. As a consequence the digits 00 may be read as 1900 and not 2000. The effect on each system is unpredictable and systems may close down causing problems with equipment. Examples to look for are power plant failure, dams flooding, natural gas failure, etc. We need your assistance to identify any major problems experienced locally, so we can assess the seriousness, priority and respond correctly. The call centers listed below will be ready to take your messages. I stress, only life threatening incidents will be dealt with.

Please pass this message on to other Hams.

Thank you for your co-operation.

Contact centers

    Baker 165.7875 USSS Field Offices VIP Security

    Charlie 165 3750 USSS Field Offices Command Post

    Golf 166 4000 USSS Field Offices"

Kishwar read the text and could find no issue with it. She was heavy hearted because this preparedness could not be repeated throughout the world. Some locations were already experiencing tragedy and even perhaps loss of life. Furthermore even this tactic may have a limited effect. She felt helpless instead of optimistic and because of this desperateness quickly approved the communique. The ball was rolling now, but was it too little, too late; her thoughts meandered through all the facets of the problem but still no inspiration shone through the fog of incomprehension.

She stared at the fax unseeingly suddenly feeling drained and empty. Her unconscious mind took over requesting her assistant to retype the message on UN letterhead and send it to all countries capable of receiving it. She feared there would be all too few.

She also alerted the Commander of UN troops. "We have no defined strategy yet so you will just have to cope with the HAM messages as you see fit until communication lines have been re-established," she told him, embarrassed that they were ill prepared for this problem.

"The strategic positioning of Navy ships and the use of AWACS will help eventually," she said confidently, but felt that the uncertainty was nerve-racking. She never felt such a feeling of helplessness and subconsciously began praying.

CHAPTER 25

Raymond and Sally lay on the bed in each other's arms, hoping that this time would last forever. Sally was in a playful mood and was teasing Raymond unmercifully at his sudden thrust into unwanted fame.

"Not only did you bypass your boss! But your bosses boss! Your Majesty." She could not resist taunting him.

"It was a one off conversation" he contested, "a freak chance, it will never happen again."

"Don't count on it, big shot, you'll be invited for coffee at the White House next, for saving the world," she teased

"Cut it out!" he snapped back unable to equate her words to his confused feelings.

He wondered just how his name got in front of the President. It was unlike Pagano to even share the credit, let alone pass it down the ranks. The more he thought about the call, the stranger he felt about it. Sally only increased his discomfort by her persistent joshing. He was still too tired to really think straight and especially to defend himself against Sally's mocking derision.

"These last twenty four hours have been unbelievable" he threw back at Sally without thinking,

"You're telling me buster, I was happily ploughing through my mundane life until you called, now I'm with the President's best friend! I wouldn't be surprised if you were under surveillance now that you are a VIP!"

"Aw! stop it! Will you? The President has already forgotten my name," he pleaded.

I'll bet you'll forget me soon" she laughed throwing her head back playfully. She was enjoying herself immensely at Raymond's expense; it was a way to relieve the tension and disappointment of the last six hours.

Raymond knew his passive manner would not cut it so he went on the attack. "I understand your jealousy Sally but there's no need for it, I'll tell the President about you the next time we talk!" It was hard for him to keep a straight face.

"You pompous ass!" she shrilled, taken aback by his change of tactics "I don't need your help to get recognized, I got nominated for this job before you and if I remember correctly it was me that suggested that you could help by recognizing McKenzie, which you couldn't." She had really taken the bait and he pressed on enjoying the upper hand now.

"Come! Come! Sally, who actually discovered and solved the problem?" he asked in a serious tone, biting his tongue to keep from laughing.

Her face was priceless now, shocked, beautiful, quizzical, and speechless and he looked lovingly at her. He never noticed the contortion of her features into unbridled rage, her face flushed beet red and she gasped for air trying to get the words out.

"You son of a bitch!" she sneered, "Your arrogance is unbelievable, without me you would still be in your dingy little office, lost in your tiny little world." She swung her legs over the side of the bed and pulled on her panties, forgetting her bra, she slipped into her dress.

"Sally, Sally." Raymond tried to interrupt

"Get lost you loser!" She was inconsolable now making for the door "stay away from me you hear...." Her eyes narrowed disapprovingly at him.

The radio interrupted her last words and the White House communications officer was on line again. "Mr. Bennett, the President would like to talk to you sir, come in? Please adjust to frequency Yankee 162.6875 or Zulu 171.2875, repeat Yankee 162.6825 or Zulu 171.2875."

The message startled him; he leapt over to the radio and acknowledged the change of frequencies to the White House operator. Yankee and Zulu frequencies were assigned to the White House Communication Agency for official business and were linked directly to the presidential telephone.

"Serious stuff," Raymond thought as he felt Sally's eyes boring into his back

The President was connected immediately. "Bennett" he said sternly.

"I guess once you're part of the inner circle the niceties are gone," Raymond's mind turned over.

"I need your help to get an important message out to this Ham network of yours, immediately."

"Yes Sir," Raymond voice was hoarse.

"You know the nature of the message and we need to impress its importance. We need it disseminated throughout the country for these Hams to be our eyes and ears reporting on disasters and threatened disasters. Understand?" The president continued before Raymond could answer.

"We are using our military bases to collect the information and we only want major issues!"

"Yes Sir!"

"I'll let my aide dictate the actual message and leave it in your hands!" He signed off abruptly.

The aide came on and dictated the approved message. It was all over in three minutes. Raymond gasped in relief as the set went dead.

Sally stood there, incredulous, her fury simmering now, tinged with curiosity. He sat facing the radio not daring to face her and could predict the very words she was building up to say. It was only a matter of time.

"I'll tell the president about you the next time we talk" she mimicked mockingly. "The President and I will solve this one, Just leave it to me, Sir. No there's no one else that matters, Sir." Her sarcasm was caustic.

"Aw Sally, cut it out," he shouted. "I'm as bewildered as you, I don't know what's happening."

She was not going to let him off the hook, her rage returned. Standing up he turned to face her, both of them wanted this silly charade to stop, but were unable to find any common ground or the right words. He stepped over to her, but she backed away, looking tentatively at the floor. There was an awkward silence developing between them, so he quickly reached over to her and grabbed her arms; she was caught unaware and did not resist. He slowly put his arms around her and gently pressed his lips against hers. They kissed for a long time and all the tenderness they felt for each other flooded back. It was beautiful moment. Their lips separated and Sally smiled her cheeky smile.

"Everyone has the right to be an asshole but you abuse the privilege."

They fell about laughing.

Sally bounced back and bubbled "You start your radio chain going and I'll make coffee" she was out the door and going down stairs before he could reply. Raymond moved over to the radio set with a gleam in his eye, which meant he had already departed to some unknown location.

His first call was to old friend Bill Jobs in California who he had not spoken to in years. The two men exchanged news like kids, happy at the renewal of their friendship. They had been in school together and had kept in contact with each other since Raymond left for Boston. Raymond read from the script, not really needing to, but he felt he should comply with his Commander in Chief's' order.

Bill listened intently, not entirely convinced.

"Heard of any unusual incidences, Bill?" Raymond queried him.

"Not much today, but a buddy of mine in Anchorage received a chilling message from Uelen, in Russia, about loss of power and heat in temperatures forty degrees below," he paused and shivered at the thought of it. "But that's all," he added. "I'll get started, and ride the airwaves to history, take care!"

"You also!" Raymond said and signed off. "The chain has started," he murmured to himself. Raymond's next call was to an old contact in Maine, to whom he had talked but never met. The conversation was similar to the last one, as was the result.

"That's the two coasts covered," he thought.

He called a friend in Canada and one in Puerto Rico. "That will get things going," he said to himself and sat back for a moment to collect his thoughts. His last call was to Jon in Australia, he was more than curious to find out his fate.

Jon came over as groggy and in some pain. He had been not long released from the hospital where his right hand had been put in plaster. He had been asleep helped by the effects of painkillers and a couple of glasses of scotch. Jon began his story, laughing at his humorous episode, which emphasized the stupidity of amateurs.

Jon finalized his story, "When the police eventually did arrive at Dock Street it was not because of the fraud, but because some neighbors had reported a disturbance. Both Kelly and I were arrested for fighting and thrown into jail. No one believed my story and there was no record of your boss's call." He laughed again. "The only thing that saved me was that I remembered that the girl's handbag containing a gun had fallen out of the window into the garden when Kelly had attacked me. By the time the police investigated that statement, a call from Canberra verified my story and I was released to hospital." Jon cringed at the thoughts of the hospital. "Kelly has been detained in Sydney somewhere, there was only minutes between Kelly's potential release and his incarceration, luck was with the good guys."

Raymond related his tale and they both exchanged "war stories" in between laughter. It was strange, but both men felt very comfortable with each other as if an unseen bond tied them together.

Jon mentioned that the jail in Sydney was coping with a riot when the doors opened automatically at midnight freeing most of the prisoners. They both laughed at the thought conjured up in their own minds. They both were quiet for a moment, then Raymond asked where Jon had originally come from and Jon reached deep for his memories of New Jersey

"New Jersey," Jon murmured.

"Really!... You don't sound like it! Where in New Jersey?" Raymond was curious.

"Newark!" Jon laughed indifferently, "Not the best place in the world!"

"Where? Where? In Newark?" Raymond stammered, his voice became strained and he fought back the bile that rose in his dry throat. His tongue seemed to fill his whole mouth as he thought about the desperate possibility he was now contemplating.

Jon was in too much pain to see where the conversation was leading to and replied nonchalantly. "State Street Orphanage, way back when!"

Raymond heard the words but did not believe his ears; his mind was swimming in a state of confused suspension. He was fighting some very strange emotions of hope, grief, disbelief, and fear, which swirled about him throwing him off balance.

" When ...when were you there?" Raymond gasped

" Late seventies to early eighties!' Jon was becoming bored with the questions and had no idea where this conversation was leading.

"Where do you come from?" Jon asked Raymond, almost casually.

Raymond couldn't answer, tears were in his eyes, and he was close to sobbing uncontrollably. "Jon! Jon! This is Ray!" He could hardly form the words 'I'm Ray...Ray your brother!" he was crying and gasping for breath. A steel strap seemed to be tightening around his chest restricting his breathing and his talking.

Jon could not understand him, "What did you say, Raymond?"

"Jon I'm your brother," Raymond felt that someone else had spoken the words, he felt detached from what was happening.

Jon fell silent, unable to understand Raymond at all.

"Jon I'm Ray, I was in State Street orphanage and taken away when I was eight."

The airwaves went silent for a full thirty seconds, only the sound of gentle sobbing broke the spell. The two brothers just cried tears of joy, tears of guilt, tears of sadness, flooded together as they both realized the magnitude of their discovery.

CHAPTER 26

Ray could hardly believe the last twenty-four hours leading up to the finding of his brother. A long night at work, an unbelievable set of problems, some chance call to Tom Ricer, a random enquiry about Jon, several brief conversations, then bam!

"This cannot be true, It must be a dream," he thought repeatedly. They bombarded each other with questions and then Jon told his story for the first time.

After Raymond had left the orphanage Jon had become a loaner, almost reclusive, for several years. He became moody and never mixed with the kids, either at school or the orphanage. Jon's life was a lonely one; his only pleasure was hanging around the deli on the corner of Liberty Street and Lafayette Street, near the orphanage. The owners, Franco and Marco paid him a few dollars to run errands and fed him more often than not. He delivered food to nearby houses and offices and had two main customers. One was Sam Walsh, a retired Merchant Marine, who lived above the deli and the other was Maria Gonzales, a mother of two small children who lived at the end of Lafayette Street.

"Jon, run this down to Gonzales as soon as possible!" Mario instructed him, "this broad never has anything in to feed those kids," he sounded concerned.

Jon took the package and ran the hundred yards to number 339 Lafayette. Maria answered the door. She looked older than her twenty-six years; her dark brown hair was stringy and usually unkempt. She constantly had bloodshot eyes and dark rings under them, and hardly wore make-up, but was not unattractive. Her slim waist and long legs made her fashionably skinny. She lived with her two daughters, aged four and two. They seemed to be the main reason for her frequent bad temper.

No one knew where the father was.

"Thanks Jon" she smiled weakly, as he handed the groceries to her.

"No problem! Anytime," he stuttered.

Sam Walsh's life was the sea until he had a leg amputated several years ago. Some heavy cargo moved and crushed him while he was inspecting it, effectively ending his career. He was about forty five years old and rented a small room above the deli, which was all he could afford on the compensation, he received. Getting down the stairs with one leg was difficult, so Sam confined himself to his room, either watching television or listening to chatter on the HF radio. He loved talking on the radio, it was his only real interaction with the outside world, and it constantly reminded him of the places he had been and the people he had seen.

His only regular visitor was Jon, who brought up his dinner from the deli almost every night. It was a good relationship, the owners of the deli rented him the room and they threw in some food. Jon enjoyed visiting Sam and listen to his stories about the sea and the foreign countries he had visited. His tales were enhanced when they listened to the jabbering on his Kenwood high frequency radio, which captured conversations from all over the world. The two became great friends and Sam taught Jon how to use the radio, telling him about the HAM network and showing him, on maps, where the countries and cities were. Jon also learned about shipping routes, trading partners and foreign customs from Sam who made a geography lesson much more interesting than any dreary schoolteacher.

At fifteen years old Jon began babysitting for Maria's kids, it was easy enough as they were always in bed when he came and rarely got up. Maria was always home by ten thirty to let Jon beat curfew at the orphanage. His only taste of home life was between Maria and Sam and he made the most of it. Friday and Saturday evenings were his favorite time to baby-sit as he enjoyed watching the weekend movies without the interruptions at the orphanage.

One Saturday, late in October he sat watching Midnight cowboy on the television, the kids were in bed. He was intrigued by the movie, the time passing fast, only an hour to go before Maria returned. He heard the front door open and Maria staggered in cursing in Spanish about her date. As soon as she entered the room he could see she was angry.

"Mama Mia, that son of a bitch" she said to no one. She made her way unsteadily to the kitchen and poured herself stiff vodka. "Jon!" she called out "Never get involved with anyone, they're all shit!" she spat the last word out. Maria staggered over to the sofa and sat down beside Jon unsteadily.

"What's on?" she slurred, as she squinted at the television.

"Midnight Cowboy," Jon replied, looking at her out of the corner of his eye.

"You naughty boy, you're too young for this!" She looked at him coyly.

"Sixteen is not too young for this," Jon said matter of fact. "Are you alright?"

"I'm never alright when it comes to men, they're shit!" the last word was emphasized again.

Jon was unsure whether to leave her in this state, but felt uneasy.

"I'd better leave," he said sitting on the edge of the sofa.

"O.K. O.K!" Maria tried to stand "I'll get your money" she stood up momentarily, drink in hand and fell sideways, landing on top of Jon sending him backwards on the sofa. The vodka followed her lead and covered him also. She tried to push herself up, putting her hands all over him. In her last attempt, her hand found his crotch, swollen now from her touch.

His face flushed in embarrassment. She stopped trying to get up and looked at him, smiling at his discomfort, she started teasing him, thrusting her breasts into his face.

"Jon, I'm surprised at you!" She laughed.

He tried to get her off of him, but his futile attempts only made matters worse. His emotions were confused, he was aroused but felt afraid, guilt surfaced along with desire. He stopped struggling.

"Let's make a man of you tonight!" her smile was wicked, the alcohol numbed her conscience

She pinned him down on the sofa, her legs straddled his body as she sat up, and removed her shirt and bra. He had seen a woman's body before, in an old Playboy magazine, but this was his first real encounter. Jon lay still and succumbed to Maria's drunken seduction. He liked the experience but was glad it was over, and he left Maria snoring on the couch.

Jon continued to babysat for Maria with one change. After the girls were put to bed Maria did not go out, and Jon became known as the "Midnight Cowboy." Despite Maria's attentions Jon found his life unbearable. Through Sam he had developed the urge to see the world and desperately wanted to begin the adventure. Sam sensed his unrest and even encouraged it.

"You should spread your wings as soon as possible," he advised, "Get out of this rat hole and make something of yourself, try and get your hands on your birth certificate from the orphanage, and we'll see what we can do," Sam said. Jon waited patiently for the right moment and "borrowed" the certificate; he photocopied it and returned the copy to the office. Sam copied the original again carefully and altered his birth year, aging him two years, old enough to join the Navy, and also changed his name from "Davies" to "David." He photocopied the changed version and put it into an envelope.

In the summer of 1989 Sam made one of his rare excursions outside of his apartment. Jon carried his crutch as Sam sat on the top stair and sat on each subsequent stair as he moved downwards. Supported by Jon he slid into a waiting taxi. The destination was a shipping company.

Sam growled at the Cab Driver, "Blue Star Line, in Elizabeth, New Jersey."

The cab moved off and forty minutes later pulled up in front of a large old building. Jon helped Sam into the reception area and he asked to see Steve Finley. Steve appeared fifteen minutes later, his large grizzled face was genuinely pleased to see Sam and they embraced like brothers. After a pleasant thirty minutes of reminiscing, Sam gave Steve Jon's new birth certificate. Fifteen minutes later, Jon and Sam left the office, just as a cab pulled up. Jon was clutching instructions to report to his first ship, *The Star of Miami*, in two days.

It was a melancholy two days for both of them filled with excitement for the future and sadness for the present. Sam tried to prepare Jon for the work ahead as best he could and constantly questioned his own judgment about helping Jon escape his mundane present. Jon did not tell anyone he was leaving.

Two days later Sam ordered a taxi. Jon once again helped him downstairs and they stood on the sidewalk. Sam hugged him, and then pushed five twenty dollar bills into his coat pocket. Jon looked across to the orphanage and remembered the day Ray had left, with his one shabby suitcase. Today he looked down at his worn out school bag; his eyes misted over, as he walked toward the taxi.

"You take care of yourself!" Sam stood with tears in his eyes.

"I will!" Jon sobbed, unable to look at Sam. His thoughts fluctuated between Sam and Raymond his lost brother, as he sat in the rear seat of a dilapidated yellow cab. The car accelerated down the street and he wondered why he had been chosen to handle so many indignities, the tears flowed freely.

The Star of Miami was a new fifty thousand-ton container ship. It had modern facilities and pleasant surroundings but life aboard was hard for Jon. He seemed to be at everyone's beck and call. The days were torturously long and the nights short and noisy. His first assignment was with the engineers, carrying tools and running errands. The ship's two engines were monitored electronically by microchips embedded into the machinery, which alerted the engineers, via warning lights, when problems arose. Few problems were unanticipated consequently the engineers were never really stretched, and had time to teach him about mechanics and electronics, and even programming. He was a quick study and enjoyed learning new skills, however, he could never get used to being in the bowels of the ship away from the sunshine and fresh air.

Jon worked for Blue Star for two years sailing mainly between Miami and Caracas, Rio de Janeiro, South America. Occasionally they visited the Caribbean islands which everyone looked forward to.

During a brief visit to Puerto Rico he met several members of a cruise ship in the "Black Angus," one of San Juan's more notorious haunts .The tales got taller as the drinks flowed but they convinced Jon that cruising was the only life at sea. Bored with the "Star" he now craved the action of a floating hotel.

It took three months and a stroke of luck before he joined the *Ocean Venture,* a cruise ship based out of Miami, sailing to Jamaica, Dominican Republic, and the Bahamas. He started out in the engine room and noticed little difference from his previous life. His luck changed when there was an outbreak of measles topsides, during a cruise, and he became a temporary steward. After a rocky start he soon picked up the tricks of the trade, his quiet demeanor projected him as very polite and he became popular with passengers. His sultry good looks were an asset and his muscular build a definite eye turner for the teenage girls who were constantly attracted to the shy, remote hunk. Thanks to Maria, his sexual experience gave him a worldly look beyond his years, and enhanced his desirability. There were strict rules about mixing with the passengers and Jon adhered to them fervently even though the girls made it difficult. The most common trick was to call him to the cabin, on a ruse, then come out of the bathroom naked, wearing only a false look of surprise.

These incidents were a constant challenge to him; temptation wrestled with his conscience and his conscience usually won out.

Two years passed quickly and Jon was truly happy for the first time in his life, content with his work, he at last felt part of something worthwhile. He particularly liked the Christmas period when the ship was at capacity, everyone was a little more considerate, and time glided by, as fast as the sea under the bow of the ship. The first port of call, in the Christmas itinerary, was Puerto Rico and nineteen ninety-three was no exception. Jon's spirits were soaring in anticipation of visiting his favorite Port, when he was unexpectedly summoned to one of his duty cabins, occupied by two eighteen-year-old girls. They requested a change of bed linen under the pretence that they had spilled soda on the old ones. Jon knocked and slowly entered the cabin with the sheets over his arm. He showed surprise when he noticed one of the girls in bed and backed out of the room.

"Shall I come back?" he asked, avoiding looking at her.

"No, come in!" she said, and wrapped the blanket around her. Jon made for the empty bunk and began to change the sheets. He noticed the girl stand up; the only thing she wore was a smile. He turned to leave but was blocked by a second girl, who came out of the bathroom. The girls were obviously sisters, strikingly beautiful with long blond hair and striking green eyes, which challenged his manhood. Their bodies were perfect, gently muscular with small breasts, narrow hips and long legs.

"Relax," the girls spoke in unison, determined to break his resistance. He had no room to move in the small cabin, they began to caress and undress him slowly. This provocation was extreme and Jon knew the temptation was too great for him to resist, he could not pull himself away and slowly became an active participant in their games. The blissful experience lasted more than an hour and was as unforgettable as it was unfortunate. The stories and "Polaroid's" went around the ship like wildfire and he was dismissed summarily when the ship docked the next day, in San Juan.

It took two weeks before he picked up another cruise ship visiting Puerto Rico from Greece, via Tenerife. Life continued much the same as the last two years. He found that Europeans were much less inhibited and more determined to bed him. He decided not to fight them too much and it was only a matter of time before he was beached again, this time in Athens. His reputation now prevented him from working with a cruise line so he signed up on an oil tanker, "The Oskar" and shipped out to the Far East running oil between Saudi Arabia and Japan. He found himself back in the engine room, which reminded him of his first job with the *Blue Star Line*, which now seemed like decades ago. Along with memories, discontentment resurrected itself and he desperately looked for a way out of this self-destructive life.

His chance came when "The Oskar" was routed to Sydney,

Australia for repairs. During the five-day stay Jon fell in love with the historic city and picture perfect harbor. On the fifth day he watched the ship edge its way out of Sydney's harbor, from the safety of the Opera House. He wore a self-satisfied smile on his face.

Jon roamed the dock areas for several days and eventually got a job in a small boatyard, which designed and built luxury yachts. Although computer aided design was heavily utilized in the boatyard, Jon found that his practical knowledge of mechanical engineering and electronics was very useful and he began to suggest viable modifications. He enjoyed the challenge of learning a new skill and soon became adept at computer aided design, his reputation grew so much that he joined the team which designed the yacht that brought the America's cup to Freemantle.

Life was good in Australia, Jon finalized his tale.

Raymond had listened in awe at Jon's story; his life now seemed tame in comparison.

CHAPTER 27

Raymond checked his watch, 5.36p.m. Hawaiian time. "They will be well into their celebrations now," he mused. He had been working now for twenty-six hours and looked like it. Worse than that he felt like it. He was listless, too tired to do anything, yet too alert to sleep. He paced in and out of the kitchen, picking up any reading material he could get his hands on, tossing it down soon after. His restlessness began to infuriate Sally,

"Find something to occupy your mind!" she said irritably.

Raymond walked into the hall and on impulse leapt upstairs where he called Jon again, it was late afternoon in Sydney on January 1, 2000, and the new millennium was now over sixteen hours old.

"How's everything downunder?" Raymond asked lazily.

"Chaos, pure chaos," Jon responded. "Communication is poor, but I've heard rumors that all flights in Australia have now been cancelled. The few flights that did make it, experienced severe difficulties in landing, taxing, disembarking and refueling, crazy eh?" Jon laughed weakly. "The passengers could not get their baggage and apparently the customs and immigration process was a joke.

"I hope that is all!" Raymond interrupted.

"Nope! Gas is difficult to get due to power outages and pump failures, worse still; telephones are erratic so we don't know the full extent of the problem. Emergency services are having difficulties in communications and therefore prioritization."

"Anything serious?" Raymond asked."

"Rumor has it that some coal miners are trapped underground due to the failure of the mine shaft elevators, don't know much about it but if they don't get air!" Jon did not finish his sentence.

"Also water pumping is erratic, which could be serious over the long-term," his tone became serious. "It really caught us out and I hear from Tom that New Caledonia is not much better," he added.

Sally joined Raymond, kissed him on the back of the neck and sat down beside him, in front of the radio. Raymond spoke into the microphone; a smile crept over his face. "Jon! I would like you to meet Sally, she works for Global Insurance and is tracking down the bad guys!"

"Hi Sally! He keeping you busy over there?"

"You bet!" Sally was smiling unconsciously. "I have to do everything and he gets all the credit, he didn't know whether to call you or the President just now!"

"The President!......the President of what?" Jon sounded amused.

"The President of the United States of America," Sally said very slowly, a slight edge to her voice.

"Let's not get into that one again!" Raymond pleaded.

"Must be an in joke!" Jon caught the drift of the conversation.

"Nothing really," Raymond tried to end it.

"Don't believe him, Jon, he and the President are good buddies now, he can ask for anything."

"Um! Sounds like my family is important!" Jon again.

"Yes, a veritable VIP!" Sally was enjoying joshing Raymond again especially with her new found ally.

"I wonder what's ahead of us now?" Raymond interjected; a serious tone had crept into his voice.

"Who knows? It's for the big boys to take care of, that is what they are paid for, if we had screwed up so badly we would have been fired, immediately. They are lucky we came along to help them!" Jon sounded edgy. "What are you two planning now?" He asked casually.

"We are staying here for a few days," Sally interjected, grabbing Raymond's arm for comfort. "Courtesy of the 'ILA' who have paid for this lovely house!" she added.

"Yeah, this place is great!" Raymond interrupted. "We'll hang about for as long as we can," he looked at Sally and they both giggled.

"It's a tough break!" Jon laughed out loud. "Sure is, I just hope I don't get too used to it," Raymond again. "It does not get much better than this."

"Well make the most of it! Sounds like it will be all up hill after this!" Jon sounded prophetic.

"We will, Raymond has promised to wait on me hand and foot!" Sally joked.

"Sure!" Raymond smiled, "But you'll be paying for the servants." They all laughed again. The jokes and laughter continued effortlessly among the three of them and it became obvious to Jon that Raymond and Sally were head over heels in love. The giggles, taunts, and laughter came over the airwaves like a wedding invitation.

"It's so obvious you two should get married, why don't you use this time as a honeymoon." Jon blurted out, jokingly

Raymond turned to Sally and momentarily her eyes said it all, she looked demurely downwards focussing on the floor her cheeks gently flushing. Raymond leant over and kissed her gently. He turned to the radio

"It's a deal!" he shouted. "On one condition! You are the best man," Raymond surprised Jon. There was a short silence.

"No trouble at all," Jon was laughing, " I'll book the next flight out immediately, see you when the planes start flying again!" He continued to joke.

"Don't do that!" the newly engaged couple echoed.

"It's still too early to fly on scheduled aircraft, you will never make it." Sally said gravely. "Raymond will use his new found VIP status to get you here," she giggled again.

Jon signed off convinced that it was all just wishful thinking.

The joke had become serious and Raymond concentrated on the task at hand, his restlessness had disappeared, as he tried to break Washington's red tape and arrange a very special flight.

It took a few hours to get clearance, but when Jon reached the air base just outside Sydney, he realized it was no joke. He was greeted be the Australian Air Force brass and loaded into a RAAF Harrier jet, for the first leg of his journey. Within minutes the jet took off vertically and at two hundred feet slowly turned Northeast towards Noumea in New Caledonia. One hour and forty minutes later, now joined by Tom Ricer, they were boarding an experimental four-seater Phantom IV supplied courtesy of the U.S. Navy. This aircraft was developed to photograph both the constellations above and seas below to determine any correlation between planetary movement and severe storm activity. In theory this data could be used to predict future weather patterns. Besides the two pilots the plane had room for two observers whose job it was to simultaneously monitor conditions above and below the flight path.

It was drizzling as Jon and Tom approached the Phantom IV aircraft surrounded by local security people. A young looking man in a jump suit walked forward to welcome them. Tom turned to Jon

"It doesn't look very big," his eyes showed his nervousness.

"Hello Gentlemen, I am your pilot, Chuck Reynolds," he held out his hand to both of them in turn.

Tom shook his hand asking "Enough room for four in there?"

"Yes sir" came the polite reply.

Jon took his hand "You logged many hours in these?"

"Yes, sir about two hundred." The young pilot turned and led them to the plane.

The co-pilot, equally young looking, fitted both of them with a flight helmet and shoed them to their cramped seats.

"How long will the flight take?" Tom asked.

"Depends on the weather conditions, our ETA is in approximately three hours," came the official sounding reply, taking Tom back to his Navy days.

"How many miles is it?" Tom again nervously

"About four thousand!"

"Jesus!" Tom said, "that's over a thousand miles an hour."

"About fifteen hundred!" the co-pilot said, calmly.

Tom looked at Jon, raised his eyebrows and silently prayed.

Jon found it difficult to get seated due to the Plaster on his arm, but his seat behind the co-pilot gave him a great view of the heavens. It was also a tight squeeze for Tom whose age had brought with it a larger waistline. He sat in the belly of the plane looking at the ground. Both passengers felt cramped surrounded by the latest in technological development of cameras, computers, and digital maps.

A humming noise filled the cabin as the crew began turning on the switches. Slowly the plane rolled to the head of the runway. Jon and Tom had experienced the roughest of seas in their seafaring careers and were not prone to motion sickness but neither was prepared for the takeoff and rapid climb of the Phantom. At 10,000 feet, Tom threw up in the bag given to him giving his insides a little relief from the nausea. Jon fought desperately to keep his insides inside him. There was little initial chatter over the plane intercom as the pilots concentrated on their climb to sixty thousand feet. After fifteen minutes Captain Reynolds leveled off at cruising altitude at just fewer than sixteen hundred knots.

"I understand this trip is of national importance?" Reynolds questioned his passengers carefully.

"You could say that son," Tom replied, laughing to himself.

Jon jumped in and summarized their story, adding that he hoped that this plane was Y2K compliant. The Pilots were impressed by the tale Jon and Tom related and relaxed; knowing a little more about their passengers dissipated the mysteriousness and tension of their mission. They were Gulf War veterans and exchanged tales about their experiences in the Middle East fascinating the passengers about the smart bombs and spying missions they had been on.

"Looks like we may be going back," Reynolds said evenly.

"What brought you out here?" Tom asked inquisitively.

"We were searching for a foundering freighter!" Reynolds again. "The Tonami," he added.

"What's its status?" Tom inquired enthusiastically.

"They lost power at midnight and drifted for two hours towards the Minerva Reefs."

"Um," Tom added his murmurs to the humming noises of the plane.

"When we arrived an old engineer had just bypassed the electronics and restored power to one screw." "They'll make it!" Reynolds added.

Tom shouted through the intercom to Jon, "Hear that?" that's one mystery solved eh!"

"Great that it ended well!" Jon added.

With the newly found relaxed atmosphere the pilots showed Jon and Tom what the plane really could do, much to Tom's discomfort. At 12 miles high, Jon was not too enthusiastic about the rocket like maneuvers the aircraft was capable of. In one dive the plane neared MACH III speed.

"Hell Jon, you see the curvature of the earth," Tom marveled.

"Something to tell our children!" Jon chuckled, fighting to hold on to his consciousness.

The pilots levelled the plane off then vectored for Maui travelling at over Mach II. The Hawaiian Islands came into view two and three quarter hours into the flight, so quickly in fact that the passengers could hardly believe it. The Phantom's nose dipped and the rapid descent began.

"Here we go again!" Tom sounded pensive; he began to feel nauseous again.

The final leg into Wailuku was hell for Tom; he now had nothing, left to throw up, and found himself praying for the torture to end.

A second visit by the world's most advanced aircraft caused more of a stir at the small airport than before. The noise brought the small airport to a standstill as onlookers stopped to stare at the unrecognizable shapes, rapidly decelerating down the runway. Something special had happened this day, but no one had any idea what and they just made a mental note to look for reports of the incident in local newspapers.

The jet taxied rapidly to the end of the runway and was met by an unmarked police car amidst strict security. The wing lights of the plane and car headlights pierced the darkness, creating an eerie scene; the two passengers stretched their cramped limbs.

"Man that was something," Jon said enthusiastically.

"Yeah! But I was tortured to hell," Tom added, "But I sure do admire these guys, I'm glad they're on our side!"

Tom and Jon changed out of their jump suits in a small maintenance shed and returned to thank the pilots. The shadowy figures of four men could be seen shaking hands and joking in a gesture of mutual respect. Waving goodbye the pilots turned to check out their multimillion-dollar carriage and the passengers turned and walked towards the waiting police car.

Jon and Tom were impressed with Raymond's arrangements and slumped into the rear seat.

"Boy, do I feel tired!" Tom yawned.

"Me too!" Jon was squirming, trying to find a comfortable position. "This international travel has me beat."

They had crossed the International Date Line and stepped back in time; it was now only ten twenty on December 31 1999. Both men napped for twenty minutes lulled to sleep by the motion of the car, and woke up on the outskirts of Lahaina. Jacob began to relate the brief history of the Island, and Tom remembered vaguely a brief visit to Honolulu many years ago but refrained from talking about it. Jon began to feel nervous, his stomach muscles tightened involuntarily as he anticipated meeting Raymond. He began to sweat, even though the car air conditioning was on. Tom noticed Jon's distress.

"You don't look so good Jon?"

I'll be okay!" he said but his nervousness increased as the car drew up slowly to the Pink house.

Sally was in the front yard, jointly waving at the car and turning to call for Raymond, excitement clearly showed in her face. Raymond loped out of the houses, and put his arm around Sally; like Jon his face showed both tension and anticipation. The car stopped, doors were thrown open and the two passengers slid out to welcoming arms.

The next three minutes were filled with handshakes, hugs, and tears as the four strangers introduced themselves to each other. Jon and Raymond sobbed uncontrollably, locked in each other's arms. They moved towards the house en masse afraid to let go of each other in case the dream disappeared. Jacob quietly followed them into the house, he shook his head unable to understand a word that was spoken as the gang of four laughed and cried and held each other constantly.

Tom was the first to break the spell, "How about a stiff drink to wash down this smell of aviation fuel?"

"Sounds a good idea," Jon seconded the proposal.

Raymond left for the kitchen to mix the drinks while Sally and Jon remained in a bear hug of an embrace. Jacob helped Raymond bring five large glasses of whiskey.

When everyone was served Jacob raised his glass and said loudly, "To Sally and Raymond, salute!"

They raised their glasses, "To Sally and Raymond!"

The sound of clinking glasses and laughter filled the room again.

Tom raised his glass "To Raymond and Jon! May you make up for lost time!"

"Here, here," everyone echoed. Tom downed his drink and went for a refill, returning with the half full bottle.

He refilled the glasses and toasted "Millie the Millennium Bug who brought us all together"

"To Millie!" They all shouted.

Jacob looked mystified, "Who the hell was Millie?" he thought.

The reunion celebration merged into the New Year's eve celebration which in turn merged into a bachelor party.

Tom found another bottle of Bushmill's and they finished it while discussing the events of the last twenty-four hours. Jacob listened intently to the stories of the Y2K problem. His thoughts were a mixture of amazement and fear, he became unsure of what was real and what was exaggeration.

"Will Maui be involved? He asked hesitantly, uncertainty showing in his eyes, he remembered the problem experienced when Honolulu was blacked out in a test in nineteen ninety-eight.

"Almost definitely!" Raymond assured him. His smile belied his seriousness.

"Yeah! You should prepare for it," Jon added, lifting his glass again, "If it's not too late," he added.

"What will happen?" Jacob was pensive, trying to decide what was real, and what was fiction.

"The main problem will be lack of communication, I think, perhaps some panic in hotels with a lack of power, elevator stoppages, credit card authorization hiccups etc.," Raymond said, a tone of authority in his voice, subtly mixed with slurring.

"In Australia we suffered from disabled traffic lights, and difficulty in getting gas," Jon added. "Also all flights were cancelled." He laughed uncontrollably at this fact; the effects of the whiskey were becoming visible.

"Are you kidding me?" Jacob queried; Panic welled up inside of him; he was unable to comprehend how his life was going to change in a few short hours.

"No, take this seriously, Jacob." Raymond tried to be somber, fighting the effects of the whiskey. "It's better to be prepared anyway!" Raymond added.

"Will you help?" Jacob gave a long solemn look of exasperation.

"Any way we can!" Sally, intervened. She was the most sober and the most credible.

Jacob thought for a moment, the others continued drinking, remaining silent for a while. He finally spoke. "Will you brief my men on the subject, so they can be more effective? This is unknown to us, such an occurrence!" he sounded alarmed.

"Of course!" Raymond was enthusiastic, verging on happy. "Bring them here and we will explain to them what may happen!" He lifted his glass and finished his drink, uncertain if his sentence had made sense to anyone.

Jacob walked out to his patrol car and radioed his dispatcher, "Send all available personnel to the pink house, O.K! 12 Orchard Street, Lahaina, as soon as possible, over!" He returned inside.

"I think coffee is the order of the hour," Sally said hopefully, she stood unsteadily and made her way slowly to the kitchen. Jacob followed her; he needed something to distract him from his troubles.

Several hours later Jacob and his officers left to prepare for the new millennium and it's immediate challenges. At least there would be fewer surprises, thanks to his newfound friends.

Tom, Jon, Raymond and Sally continued to party and found new hope with every new bottle they opened.

"It sure is a night to remember," Raymond said philosophically.

It was well past two thirty before they decided to sleep, or to be more correct, before sleep overcame them. Jon and Tom could hardly stand and Raymond was only in a slightly better condition. Sally was intoxicated only by her happiness and was determined to get Raymond upstairs at least to the bedroom, if not the bed. She coaxed, cajoled, and pulled Raymond upstairs. He made torturously slow progress, stopping frequently to giggle uncontrollably at some humorous thought. Once he was in the bedroom, she gave up and left him on the floor, lying halfway between the door and the bed.

"Some bachelorette party," she muttered under her breath as she threw a blanket over Ray's prone body. She undressed and slid under the covers, turning to face Raymond she listened to his breathing, and slowly fell into a deep sleep. Sally's dreams were mixed and drifted between the idyllic island setting, her upcoming wedding and her new friends. She did not know if it was excitement, or noise in the house, which caused her to wake.

"There it is again," she thought.

The stairs creaked again;

"It must be Tom or Jon moving about!" Hope mixed with fear as she lay deadly still.

Suddenly the bedroom door slowly opened, letting in a thin wedge of light. The beam grew large enough to allow a head to peer in; it was a painfully slow process, as Sally watched this theater unfold.

Raymond was still on the floor and lay between Sally and the intruder. He turned and lay on his back and began snoring loudly.

The intruding head backed out quickly then slowly re-emerged. He was taking time to assess the room, letting his inquiring eyes adjust to the darkness; he looked down at Raymond. The door opened further, now a shoulder appeared and then the top of a body.

Sally could see the dark, shadowy, figure move toward her and begin to step over Raymond. She lay still, fear choking at her throat, she felt helpless. "Raymond could never respond if she shouted out," she thought. She lay motionless, watching the intruder move toward the wardrobe, his head scanning the room constantly for movement or noise.

The figure crept to the right hand side of the wardrobe and moved it noiselessly from the wall, stopping occasionally to feel blindly behind it. He crouched down and she could hear slight scraping sounds as he dragged something from behind the furniture. Flashes of light invaded the dark room as light glinted off something reflective. Slowly the intruder retreated out the room, once again stepping over Raymond, who was in a fitful sleep now.

Sally watched the silhouette as it neared the half open door and now saw the brief case in his hand. He was half way out, when she dove from the bed and threw her weight against the door tripping over Raymond doing so. The intruder threw out a curse at the surprise of the attack and wriggled about trying to free himself from the vice like grip of the door and the wall. Raymond stirred from his drunken sleep, disturbed by the noise and Sally's weight now sprawled over him. He cursed, and tried to twist himself free causing Sally's weight to press harder against the door.

The intruder growled in pain trying to push against the door.

The noise upstairs disturbed Tom from his stupor-induced sleep, he tried to sit up but felt two hands grab at his shirt, lifting him up slightly.

"What the hell !......" his sentence remained unfinished. He felt a punch hit his jaw and he fell backwards, his head hit the floor hard, causing him to drift into semi-consciousness.

Jon remained in a deep sleep, unaware of the attacks.

Upstairs the struggle continued, the intruder backed into the bedroom flailing the brief case into Sally's side causing her to fall away from the door. Raymond had no idea what was happening, but instinctively lunged at the dark figure. He grabbed both legs and brought him crashing to the floor half inside the bedroom and half outside on the landing. He held on to both legs in rugby like tackle. Raymond felt the briefcase hit his head, he cursed out loud, but held on desperately. The two men wriggled out to the second floor hallway still locked together. The intruder used the stair rails as leverage, and began to kick Raymond hard. His head exploded in pain from the blows and he loosened his grip momentarily. The intruder freed his other leg and hauled himself vertical, helped by the stair rail. Raymond was in bad shape, stunned by the blows, bleeding and nauseated by the booze, he was lapsing into unconsciousness. He tried desperately to hold on, his driving instinct for self-preservation overcame the pain. The intruder was nearly upright and leaning heavily on the banister when Sally leaped out of the bedroom and hit him square in the torso with her shoulder. The intruder gasped, as the breath was squeezed from his lungs.

"You bitch," he screamed, as the banister gave way and he crashed down the stairs like a sack of potatoes.

The noise momentarily disturbed Tom's assailant who looked towards the stairs. Tom seized the chance to hit him square on the jaw, his early life had prepared him well for this moment and the shadowy figure slowly keeled over backward freeing Tom from his pinned position. He scrambled to his knees grabbing his assailant by the collar; he snapped a punch against the intruder's nose, splattering blood over both of them. The stranger cursed, and fell backward smashing his back of his head against the coffee table. There was a deathly silence.

Tom called out to Raymond – "You OK up there?" Sally recognized Tom's voice with relief.

"Yes!" she gasped painfully.

Tom staggered to the light switch and threw it to the on position. The brightness blinded him momentarily and slowly his eyes focussed on the two prone bodies in front of him. There was a pool of blood underneath the head of the guy he had hit and there was no movement other than the very shallow heaving of his chest. He looked up and saw Sally. She was staring down at him; her wide eyes focussed on the heap of humanity lying face down at the bottom of the stairs. Tom moved over to the body and gently straightened it out. He noticed that the right leg and left arm were broken and the face was covered with blood. He turned the torso on to its side and heard Sally sharply inhale.

She held her breath for a full fifteen seconds then exhaled the words "Its McKenzie".

"Who?" Tom was breathing heavily.

"McKenzie," she repeated, her voice was a painful whisper.

Raymond was by her side now swaying groggily. He shivered involuntarily at the thought of the chillingly close call.

"It's McKenzie" she sniffed and turned to Raymond, burying her head into his chest.

"It's over!" Raymond said hoarsely and patted her comfortingly.

They helped each other down the stairs and joined Tom, and now Jon, beside McKenzie's still body assuming the worst.

"We'd better call the police" Tom was the most coherent.

Raymond consoled Sally, holding her tight, as they looked desperately at McKenzie. Sally still had her head buried in Raymond's chest and sobbed uncontrollably;

Tom moved quietly to the phone and dialed zero for the operator. There was no dial tone. Jon knelt down and placed his ear against McKenzie's mouth. He could feel the weakest of breaths as McKenzie exhaled.

He looked over to Tom, relief showed in his eyes. "Better call an ambulance, Tom."

"No phone," Tom waved the instrument in the air in frustration.

"Better use the radio upstairs," Raymond suggested.

Sally clutched at Raymond, not daring to believe Jon's words; she kept her head buried not daring to breathe.

Jon looked at Raymond "He's alive" Raymond felt Sally shiver and heard the gasp of air, as she left consciousness and slipped to the floor.

CHAPTER 28

Jacob and his men came into sorry looking sight. He scanned the room. Three male drunks sipping coffee, the mugs cupped in their hands, eyes sunken in their heads and pain written all over their faces. They sat on the sofa like the three wise monkeys. One female lying on the floor, color drained from her face and glazed eyes searching for help, two unconscious's bodies lying in their own blood. Raymond and Jon tried to smile as they looked up at Jacob who strode purposefully into the lounge, stepping over McKenzie's body, which still lay at the base of the stairs.

He shook his head slowly from side to side, and rubbed his stubbly chin as he looked at his watch, 5.30 a.m. January 1.

"It's too early for this, especially after the night I've had," Jacob said wearily. "What happened?"

Raymond was the first to offer Jacob an explanation. Looking drawn and exhausted he stood up, swayed a little.

"This is McKenzie," he rasped pointing at the prone body near the bottom of the stair, his voice hoarse with dehydration. He turned to the other body, "And this is his accomplice, we don't know his name yet." He looked lost after this effort and moved behind the sofa, leaning on it to steady himself. "They came for this brief case," he added picking up the black leather object. He offered it meekly to Jacob, who was still looking at the two bodies.

Jacob silently took the case and set it on to of the coffee table.

"I wonder why this is important?" he muttered.

Outside, a siren announced the imminent arrival of an ambulance, which disturbed Jacob's train of thought. Brakes squealed, doors banged, as steel met steel and two attendants entered the house gingerly. They looked at Jacob for instructions.

He looked at his officers, "Mark the positions of the bodies for now! Then take them to the hospital."

The two officers drew outlines on the floor then assisted the ambulance attendants to put them onto stretchers.

"Stay with them until relieved," he ordered.

Jacob continued to direct the activity until the two injured men were removed and only he and another police officer remained.

"What on earth happened?" he inquired.

"I guess they were peeved at not being invited to the wedding!" Jon tried to joke; his head throbbed with the pain of an oncoming hangover. No one laughed.

Jacob moved over to the brief case studying it for several seconds. There were no markings on it, just a simple black leather brief case with gold colored hinges and locks. He flicked the locks, they opened effortlessly, and he lifted the lid slowly. The others gathered around peering at the contents. Inside were several other passports, strewn over the top of other papers and maps, some U.S. dollars and a black felt like, bag. Jacob picked up the passports, flicked through the pages and threw them on the coffee table. He shuffled through the other papers and after a brief examination; he looked at the others.

"Um, "Looks like pay dirt!" He dropped them on top of the passports, "These give us details of the whole plan, I think!" He looked back inside the brief case and then mistakenly picked up the black bag by the bottom. Diamonds slowly cascaded out like a glistening waterfall, and bounced into the brief case, creating a spectacular moving light show. All five stood silent staring, as if hypnotized by the sparkling movement of the light that danced before their eyes. They were still for a full half-minute.

Raymond leaned over and selected the largest diamond. He inspected it closely, then turned to Sally and said simply, "The engagement ring you never had."

They all laughed uncontrollably dissipating the tension of the last few minutes. The police constable stood and watched them, wondering what was so funny. His confused look was comical, which made them laugh all the more. Minutes passed until the contagious effects of the laughter subsided, into chuckles.

Sally turned to Jacob, "Coffee Jacob?"

"Yes please," Jacob was suddenly weary

"You constable?" she asked.

The constable looked gingerly at Jacob. "Yes please," he answered.

"How did your night go Jacob?" Jon asked.

"Terrible....terrible...." Jacob sounded tired. "But better than it could have been."

"We lost our dispatching capability around midnight, I'm not sure that it was a good or bad thing, even if we could communicate we did not have the resources to cope." He held up his hands in despair.

"You were right, some elevators automatically shut down and trapped a few people, the telephones were erratic, so we could not send immediate help. The traffic lights were useless, luckily not many people were travelling, but there were a few accidents. Bank alarms were triggered and hospitals and hotels plunged into darkness. Apart from that it was a walk in the park."

"What about Air Traffic?" Jon asked.

"No scheduled flights due until 10:00 a.m." Jacob replied.

"You got off lightly," Raymond interrupted.

"Well, that's all we know of," Jacob sat down and Sally entered with the coffee. They all sat around talking.

At 8.00 a.m. Jacob looked at his watch, "Four hours to go," he said wearily.

"Four hours to what?" Tom inquired.

"To the wedding," Jacob said, frowning slightly.

"Jesus Christ! How could we forget that!" Raymond panicked.

Jon and Tom scattered to catch some sleep, leaving Jacob to clear away the empty cups and make some calls.

Sally and Raymond disappeared upstairs to prepare for their "Big Day."

Three hours later the men reassembled at the bottom of the stairs anxiously waiting for Sally to reappear. Raymond paced around the hallway, frequently looking skyward for Sally, while Jon and Tom sat at the base of the stairs looking decidedly hung over.

A second police car arrived outside the house and Jacob went out side to make the final arrangements.

The three men were agitated; Jon tried to joke to relieve the tension.

"Talk about a shotgun wedding!" "Yeah, and police escorts helping reluctant grooms make the big commitment," Tom chuckled, though his pain.

Their laughter died away and intuition made Raymond look up, just as Sally reached the top of the stairs; she looked beautiful in her simple pink cotton dress, blond hair pinned up and a little make up covering her tanned face. Slowly she came downstairs; her eyes fixed on Raymond. A demure smile made her look breathtaking; she reached the second last stair and stood momentarily, glancing at each of the men, in turn.

"You look fabulous!" Raymond said at last

"You sure do!" Jon and Tom echoed

Jon stepped forward and took her arm, "This way my queen!"

She stepped into the hall and moved towards the front door, Raymond at her side. Jacob came in and ushered them to the waiting cars. Sally and Raymond in the first car the rest of them in the second. Both cars moved off slowly and drove sedately through town to the white wood frame church, one mile away. Local people filled the church, Islanders love weddings and with Jacob involved they knew the bride and groom must be important.

The ceremony was short; Jon fulfilled his best man duties using Tom's wedding ring donated at the last minute. It was a moving ceremony made all the more touching by its simplicity. Most of the congregation was lost in their own private thoughts of whatever was important to them. Jacob looked lovingly at his wife and family, Tom remembered his parents and thanked God for his wife. Jon remembered when he watched as Raymond was taken away from him so many years ago.

Everyone felt euphoric in this dream like setting; time seemed to stand still and good memories danced around their minds in undisturbed peace.

CHAPTER 29

"The Kuwait border is only twenty five miles away Sir"

"I know," Captain Mohamed looked at his watch, "06:20, we'll cross the border in just over an hour, then we will know if the infidels have eyes in the sky."

The column rolled on at twenty miles per hour; the troops were edgy, and constantly looked for aircraft, although the sky was clear with no sign of aircraft. As ordered the platoon had traveled North for two hours then turned South toward Kuwait, moving carefully over the bleak desert landscape.

Captain Mohamed began to feel a tinge of optimism; "Perhaps our technical people were correct after all," he muttered to his driver.

Disillusionment came quickly. Above the noise of the personnel carriers he suddenly heard the unmistakable drone of jet engines and ordered all driving lights to be extinguished.

It was too late; the jets were on them in an instant.

He saw the navigation lights of three aircraft streaking across the dark sky towards them.

They were flying very low in a purposeful way, unconcerned with antiaircraft fire. As he stared at the sky, he saw one jet bank and turn northward, parallel to the column. The other two proceeded westwards and make a slow turn a full 180 degrees and head back towards them.

After several seconds, the aircraft separated and approached the troop column again about a half a mile apart.

Mohamed stared at their navigation lights through night vision glasses; fear welled up inside of him. "Strange that combat craft would keep their lights on," he said to his driver trying to show leadership.

The jets roared towards them at a height of five hundred feet, he estimated, they were approaching them from the West and just in front of the column. Mohamed was not certain that the jets had spotted them, the shadows of the dessert did an effective job of hiding them.

He stiffened when he heard the sound of gattling guns raking the sand just east of the column.

"Bastards!" he spat out the words and dove out of the jeep. His driver leapt out of the other side and ran twenty feet before falling flat to the ground.

The sound of two thousand rounds per minute was deafening in the silence of the desert, as the barrels of the gun spun in a rotational blur. Thousands of bullets sliced through the darkness, and spat a hail of twenty-millimeter shells just ahead of the stationery column. Mohamed screamed orders and obscenities, which were lost in the noise as the jets screamed overhead. Panic engulfed the troops and they fled from their positions, leaving the column defenseless. The firing ceased as suddenly as it began the pitch of the engines changed as they began to climb slowly, returning peace to the unfriendly landscape.

Mohamed screamed orders at the troops, "Get back to the trucks, you dogs!"

The scattered troops reluctantly trudged back to their posts, stricken by fear and disbelief.

Just as the sound of the two attacking aircraft dissipated, the third screamed the length of the column, very low. The engines blotted out all other sounds, and once again the troops scattered into the desert.

Mohamed waited anxiously for the strafing to begin, this time the column would be torn to ribbons.

Nothing happened.

"Murderers!" he raised his fist to the sky as he heard the plane continue south and he watched the image of the navigation lights rapidly diminish.

"Bastards, Infidels," he shouted aimlessly and shook his fist skyward.

Silence returned, he scanned the darkness for his troops. His driver appeared beside the jeep again, Mohamed screamed at him, "the radio, give me the radio!" and began calling the second column situated about twenty miles away, due east.

"Captain Mohamed calling Major Aziz come in?

"Aziz here," the airwaves crackled.

"I've just been attacked by three allied jets, the bastards knew where we were!"

Aziz replied "Yes, we heard the salvos, "Any casualties?" Aziz asked solemnly.

"No, none, not even close, this was just a warning, they could have destroyed us easily!"

"It looks as if our technical people were wrong! They will pay dearly for this!" his words sounded vengeful.

"Yes sir!" Mohamed confirmed nervously, "Their equipment is operational, despite this computer thing!"

"Prepare to return to base," Aziz was terse now, glory was not to be theirs tonight. Embarrassment and fury had replaced their highest aspirations.

"Somebody's head will roll!" He said solemnly and signed off.

The two troop columns slowly turned northward and headed back toward Rumalia. The troops were bewildered and disheartened, the mood was grave. No one broke radio silence, not daring to notify the idiots in Baghdad that the crazy plan did not work.

The three "Blackbirds" turned northwest and climbed rapidly to fifteen thousand feet where they adopted a tight vee formation and accelerated to MACH II. They cut through the air like the head of a lethal arrow, their vapor trails formed the shaft.

"Nice Plan, Chad, I didn't think we could pull it off with this radar glitch!" Lieutenant Brett Steward complimented his wingman Chad Holler.

"We were lucky to see them really," Chad replied. "They were stupid to follow the same course as our GPS indicated before it went haywire. A little extrapolation gave us some idea but I was relieved to see their lights." "Then it was just a matter of triangulation, to identify their position in the darkness, he chuckled lightheartedly. "Anyway our margin for error was great because it was the noise that stopped them, let's only hope they stay stopped!"

The jets flew northwest toward the Mediterranean hoping that Italy would authorize emergency landing rights. If not then it would be a refueling exercise then on to the U.K.

The pilots felt good that the mission was over and slowed as they flew over Greece, sending a brief coded message to the Embassy in Athens that all was well.

Lieutenant Steward reviewed his orders, "Locate and ward off moving IRAQUI troop columns, produce as much noise as possible to bluff the opposition; no force to be used unless attacked."

"It was a desperate mission but desperate times demand desperate measures," Steward thought, "One hell of a bluff!"

CHAPTER 30

"God damn it!" President Alexander was irritated. "This is supposed to be the biggest night in a thousand years, and here we are locked in the oval office trying to figure out what's happening out there!" he gestured towards the east window, his frustration rising. He rose out of this chair and paced the room restlessly. "I can't believe this!" he spat the words out. "This power outage is getting me down already, luckily some of our auxiliaries worked." He was tired and today had not gone as he expected. His audience watched him intently, his face showed the strain of leadership, his lips were tight and his eyes were heavy lidded now.

Alexander looked around the office; it was littered with empty bottles of Dom Perignon and long stemmed glasses used to toast in the new millennium, now several hours old. There were plates with the remnants of salmon; caviar, pate and filet mignon scattered around the place. The room was hot, too hot in contrast with the extremely cold weather outside. This heat had curled the bread of the sandwiches, whose stale appearance made for a very unappetizing sight. No one ordered the room cleared.

Alexander turned to look at his staff one by one, Alex Scott, John Sloan, Hank Woodward, George Trent, Paul Wayne and Gary Powell.

"Why did this have to happen on my watch?" he thought. "Some Presidents have wars to contend with, some tangible enemy that you can visualize and fight, but this mess is unbelievable!" he stretched and inhaled loudly releasing the air with a sigh. "This enemy is everywhere and nowhere at the same time," his mind wandered again and he thought about being in this unwanted place in history.

Alexander was having trouble concentrating now. He recollected the earlier meetings, which highlighted the potential magnitude of the problem, but only half believed that it would happen. What he could not grasp was the pervasiveness and randomness of the effects and the most disconcerting thing was the loss of communication. His mind wandered back to the early part of 1998 when the A.T. & T. network went down unexpectedly and then the Panamsat satellite which disabled millions of pagers. There was chaos then, and he mused that that could have been the warning for the future they were now experiencing.

The silence in the room was becoming awkward and Alexander became aware of the strained atmosphere. He coughed self-consciously then shook himself out of his inertia.

"What is our most pressing issue to deal with?" he asked brusquely.

The staff was caught unawares and after a few seconds Paul Wayne the director of NSA jumped in.

"As you know Mr. President, I missed the earlier meetings but have been brought up to speed. From my point of view, I am worried about a breach of security by some opportunistic terrorist group, much like the IRAQUI exercise." He paused for effect. "As you know we were lucky to bluff them to return to base, at least that's what we think they did," he paused for breath then continued. "It is not only problems on foreign soil I'm worried about, his eyes darted from face to face. If terrorist groups have been planted here to blow up essential buildings or

God forbid use chemical or biological warfare agents; we would be severely hampered by our communication difficulties. A chemical attack on a subway system, similar to that in Japan several years ago, could be catastrophic for us. Our response capability may be severely reduced under these circumstances.

"Have you a recommendation?" Alexander asked, raising a fractional smile, which added to the sarcastic tone of his question.

"Yes sir, I strongly recommend that you issue a direct order that all but essential service employees remain at home until further notice. "He shuffled uncomfortably in his seat. "It's the safest way I can think of under the circumstances," he added hesitantly.

Gary Powell intervened. "How long do you think this will take Paul?"

"Until we get communications under control, but I have no real idea how many days that could be!" he sighed. "The HAM network has worked fine but it is overloaded, we have to take the pressure off somehow! We could concentrate in the large metropolitan areas like New York City, Washington D.C. and L.A. first..." he did not complete his sentence.

"That would have a catastrophic effect on industry!" Powell interrupted, "And I would hate to hazard a guess on the legal ramifications," he added gravely.

"Yes, I understand your concern but in the interest of national security I cannot think of anything else." He paused. "We cannot guard every potential target as it is and as you know we have experienced trouble with immigration systems, so I cannot say, with any certainty, that dangerous terrorists are not already here and prepared to act." He took a deep breath. "We also lost communication with Interpol about eight hours ago, so we are flying blind, so to speak!"

The Vice President spoke out. "Do you think anyone has slipped in unnoticed Paul?"

"It's hard to say Alex, but I am suspicious that the IRAQUI Troops turned back so easily perhaps it was a diversion to get someone in here. Who knows in this crazy world!"

"What would their targets be?" Alexander had regained his interest.

"We usually suspect that they would go after high profile targets such as bridges, tunnels or large buildings like the Trade Center in New York City."

"What about the panic factor?" John Sloan interjected. "If we don't have an explanation about all these unexplained occurrences when the stock market opens on Monday, we could be in for a blood bath, worse than the 1930's." Sloan looked worried. "We had enough difficulties keeping people calm when they were withdrawing their balances out of the banks and insurance companies."

"I never thought of that!" admitted Powell. "We may have severe economic instability. I suppose we could close them down temporarily, I suppose!" He sounded apprehensive.

The atmosphere in the room became somber as everyone mentally calculated their own potential paper loss in such a market crash.

Alex Scott stood up slowly. "Gentlemen, you have presented some valid arguments and we have to take immediate steps to cope. As you know we have organized and sent teams to the potential crisis areas such as Nuclear Power Stations, Dams, Airports, etc. The HAM network is giving us intelligence about problems and we are prioritizing them somehow. We must now direct the population to stay home as an extra precaution." He looked up and saw his colleagues all nodding in agreement 'Fine, lets issue the directives and get them out to the State Governors as best we can and meet back here in one hour!"

An hour later President Alexander and Vice President Scott were back in the oval office, drinking coffee, waiting for the others to return.

"We've redirected the *Constellation* to Uelen, a small Russian town in the Bering Strait, apparently they were the first to experience difficulties. There are some American and Canadian citizens there. The ship will stand off shore to provide help!" Scott informed the President casually.

"How did we know about this?"

"The HAM network, would you believe it? It's damn good."

"Unbelievable," Alexander allowed himself to smile.

"There was also a rescue involving a blazing oil rig off the Burma coast. A HAM operator picked this up also."

They both looked up as the others joined them. President Alexander moved over to the window and looked outside at the falling snow. It was cold and quiet with only the faint sounds of traffic in the distance and he stared at the darkened city. He'd never seen the White House so dark before and noted the stillness of the City.

"It's hard to believe we are in such trouble as you look outside at all this peacefulness," he spoke to no one in particular. He turned and looked at the tired men. "Gentlemen, I think we have done all we can for tonight, let's get some rest and reconvene'…his sentence remained unfinished.

A loud blast shattered the silence somewhere at the perimeter of the White House.

Alexander turned toward the window and stared hypnotically at a pair of approaching headlight speeding towards the White House. The roar of a powerful engine replaced the silence, sporadic gunfire added to the confusion. The others rushed to the window horrified at how close the vehicle was, flashes of light pierced the darkness as automatic rifles were discharged. The vehicle was about fifty yards away coming directly at them when Sloan grabbed the President and threw him to the floor.

"Down, Down!" he screamed. "Move back from the window!"

All seven men fell hard on the blue carpeted floor then crawled towards the door. They heard a terrific blast, and a second later the outer wall of the office collapsed. Glass and masonry showered the prone bodies, paralyzing them with fear. Gunfire filled the air and the sounds seemed to move closer to them. Sloan shook his head vigorously to get his mind in gear; he looked around the darkened room. His eyes slowly adjusted to the sudden darkness.

"Mr. President! Mr. President, are you ok?" He heard the heavy clicking sounds as masonry fell against masonry.

Alex Scott called out "Who is ok?"

Sloan answered and he heard the voices of Woodward and Powell.

"Let's get out of here!" Sloan barked, it was like an order.

Gunfire was very close now and panic welled up inside the four men. They knelt among the debris trying to get close to the other three injured people. Sloan grasped at a body; his hands felt a warm sticky fluid. He recoiled at the touch of blood. Half standing and half kneeling he grabbed the torso and began to drag it out of the room. It was freezing now and he could make out a faint light to his right. Slowly he made for the light, dragging his charge as gently as he could. He heard others scramble the same way. He reached the door and opened it gently peering out into the corridor. Light pierced the room and he saw the other three carefully carrying Wayne and Trent towards the door. He looked down and saw Alexander, blood all over his face.

Shouts and orders echoed in the stillness of the night, both inside and outside of the White House. Sloan looked beyond the others to the missing wall; he could see the rapid yellow tongue of fire as automatic rifle fire filled the room. Instinctively he dove on top of the President's body, not even sure that he was still alive. The room was splattered with the sound of ricocheting bullets.

Sloan looked up and saw a lone assassin framed in the outline of the wall that once was there. A gun began to spit out its lethal mission and he could see small puffs of dust approach him as the fatal missiles hit the bricks about ten feet in front of him.

"This is it!" he thought.

Suddenly he was deafened by the retort of another automatic rifle fire; it was only inches from him. He could smell the cordite and felt hands grabbing at him and dragging him out of the room. He lost consciousness and woke up in a corridor, still deaf, shivering both with coldness and shock. He leaned up on one elbow.

Marines formed a human wall between the president and the assassins. No one would breach this defense on the most symbolic ground in the United States. Orders were barked somewhere in the darkness, shadows scurried about purposefully amid the confusion. Sloan turned and looked at the medics working on the President, George Trent and Paul Wayne. He was overcome with a sense of safety and a deep feeling of pride as he watched American soldiers defend their country without regard for themselves. His eyes misted over as he stared blankly at the scene before him.

Sitting further away was Scott Woodward and Powell all mesmerized by the events. He lay down and again drifted from consciousness. Two hours later he woke up lying in a small cot used by the security staff, he sat up then swung his legs over the side and tried to stand. He fell back and the young marine assigned to guard him came over.

"You all right Sir?" he asked.

"Fine, just fine," Sloan said hoarsely. His throat was dry and his head throbbed with pain. "Can you get me a drink ----- and some aspirin?" Sloan asked.

"Yes, sir coffee ok?"

"That would be great," Sloan looked at him appreciatively. "How's the President?"

"He took a nasty bump on the head." The marine stepped over with the mug of coffee and some painkillers."

Sloan cupped it in his hands and sipped it slowly, then popped two pills in his mouth and took another drink!

"Also got cut badly with flying glass, he's all stitched up and cursing badly now."

"Where is he?"

"Upstairs in his quarters, his wife has banned everyone, I think Vice President Scott is temporarily in charge!"

"Where's he now?"

"Upstairs in one of the conference rooms with the others?"

"O.K. Can you take me there?" Sloan stood unsteadily, his head throbbed and he rubbed his temples gently in a futile attempt to abate the pain.

"Ouch!" he gently fingered a large bump just on the temple and above the left eye.

He followed the marine up two flights of stairs and along a short corridor to a small conference room. The soldier nodded to another marine, then knocked and slowly opened the door. Sloan walked in to find Scott and the others all looking anxiously towards him. Scott walked over.

"Thanks for the warning!" he put his hands around Sloan's shoulders and patted his back.

"How are you?"

"Bruised and tired, but other than that, I'm o.k."

"What the hell happened?"

"Well, we can't be sure but Trent thinks it was middle eastern terrorists possibly IRAQUI. Under the cover of the darkness they rammed the perimeter fence with a van and exploded it, then used a Hummer, packed with explosives, to bomb the White House. I assumed they would guess that we would be here all night with all the problems!" Scott paused. "The scary thing was that four of them rushed the White House, guns ablaze. Some sort of Kamikaze squad to finish the job off!"

"I guess years of hatred makes desperate men!" Woodward interrupted.

"Well I hope we can assume that further terrorist attacks are not likely!" Scott looked at Wayne challengingly.

"I would not assume that Sir! Wayne said evenly. "In fact with all the confusion about this Y2K thing I suspect there may be an escalation of this sort of thing. We will have to be ever vigilant."

Scott shook his head in disbelief.

"Is there any end to this?" he asked, resentment prominent in his tone. The mood in the room was very somber.

Sloan noticed the strain in everyone's face. "What is our next step?"

"I've ordered a 'copter to take us all to Camp David, we'll set up headquarters there. We're stringing a direct line to the United Nations, to keep each other informed.

All the forces are mobilized to help and we'll react to anything that happens!"

He was interrupted by a knock on the door. A young marine entered.

"Your transport has arrived Sir!"

They were escorted out to the lawn and walked over to the aircraft, its blades still rotating, ready for lift off. Security forces were formidable now, alert to attack by snipers, helicopters, and even aircraft. Scott hesitated and looked back to the White House. One side of the building was demolished.

"We were lucky," he turned to the others with a no nonsense expression.

He appeared tired, his cheeks and chin dark with an emerging beard, his eyes black. He looked eastwards, his face stiffened and reddened for a moment then he relaxed and smiled. The sky was a light blue and the sun was like a huge orange ball half way over the horizon.

Scott took a deep breath and exhaled slowly, "Gentlemen, let's squash this Millennium Bug.